THE HANDBOOK OF INVESTOR RELATIONS

Edited By

Donald R. Nichols

Dow Jones-Irwin
Homewood, Illinois 60430

This publication is designed to provide accurate and
authoritative information in regard to the subject matter
covered. It is sold with the understanding that the
publisher is not engaged in rendering legal, accounting, or
other professional service. If legal advice or other expert
assistance is required, the services of a competent
professional person should be sought.

*From a Declaration of Principles jointly adopted by a Committee
of the American Bar Association and a Committee of Publishers.*

Acquisitions editor: Richard A. Luecke
Project editor: Jane Lightell
Production manager: Ann Cassady
Compositor: Editing, Design & Production, Inc.
Typeface: 11/13 Century Schoolbook
Printer: Arcata Graphics/Kingsport

Library of Congress Cataloging-in-Publication Data

The Handbook of investor relations/edited by Donald R. Nichols.
    p. cm.
  Includes index.
  ISBN 0-87094-966-7
    1. Corporations — Investor Relations. I. Nichols, Donald R.,
1948- .
HD59.H265 1989
658.4'5 — dc19   88–15291
                                                 CIP

Printed in the United States of America

1 2 3 4 5 6 7 8 9 0 K 5 4 3 2 1 0 9 8

INTRODUCTION

The Handbook of Investor Relations is a no-nonsense look at how corporate IR can and should be practiced with the professionalism it deserves. The essays in this volume speak to a common purpose: to specify what constitutes standards of professionalism in a discipline still searching to define itself despite having proved its usefulness.

Many of the contributors are among the foremost in their separate crafts of IR, and many others are emerging names just now being recognized for their contributions. All have something important to teach corporations and IR practitioners who sincerely want to improve their corporate postures and expand their talents.

Although this handbook consists of separate essays, it starts by showing how an effective IR program is conceived, marches through the constituencies served by IR, and ends by emphasizing corporate IR as an information-based discipline that treats its audiences with the intelligence they deserve.

Ted Pincus sets the tone in his opening essay, which discusses the evolution to date of corporate IR as a blend of intuition and information that produces measurable results.

Johnnie Johnson's essay on establishing the IR function is indispensible for corporations and practitioners who want to start or revise their IR programs.

Alyn Essman shows where the emphasis on IR properly begins — with the CEO — and his essay is followed by Peter

Lincoln's, which shows how the IR program can serve the user of financial information.

The next essays concern the constituencies of IR. They range from Bob Greer's counsel on addressing the employee-shareholder to Bea Garcia's advice on establishing credible relationships with financial media to Lou Thompson's highly knowledgeable discussion on working with government as a demanding partner in the business of informational disclosure.

Important special topics follow, and again the authors are the best in the business. Dick Cheney and Bob Taft and colleagues at Hill and Knowlton talk about the role of investor communications on both sides of merger and takeover actions. Bob Ferris proves the importance of an astonishingly slighted topic in corporate IR — the need to know who owns the corporation and votes shares. Don Kirsch is an acknowledged authority about an area of corporate capitalization that demands special attention from practitioners, the over-the-counter company.

Olha Holoyda represents one of the most vexing audiences of IR, the professional analyst, and tells practitioners why professional analysts evaluate information as they do. Marty Fridson's treatment of a neglected constituency — the bondholder — reminds every practitioner that informative IR pays returns in lower cost of capital. Earl Merkel discusses the need to make informational disclosure a comprehensive and planned communications program that addresses the audience, the media, and the message. Alan Bulmer takes the practitioner into the international arena, where the world is waiting for the IR message in capital markets.

Lee Glasner's concluding essay is the most definitive discussion yet published on standards of informational content in the MD&A of the annual report. He shows what, why, and how to give real substance to a message that management usually reduces to an invitation for readers to disregard. He presents a standard every public corporation should aspire to in its annual report.

These authors have a statement to make, and the statement is that IR can be done right. Business managers who equal the authors' convictions with their own commitment to IR will find much in this handbook to guide them to standards of real professionalism.

Donald R. Nichols

ABOUT THE EDITOR

Donald R. Nichols is managing partner of Mardon Investment Services Corporation, an investor relations consulting firm in the western suburbs of Chicago that also counsels corporations and personal investors on the use of income securities for current portfolios and pension plans. Prior to establishing his own corporation, he held investor relations responsibilities at four Fortune 500 Corporations and the nation's largest investor relations agency. *The Handbook of Investor Relations* is his fourth book for Dow Jones-Irwin and the fifth of seven investment books he will have published by the end of 1988. He holds masters' degrees in English, economics, financial journalism, and expository writing, and teaches economics at Elmhurst College.

CONTENTS

EMERGING FROM THE DARK AGES: AN OVERVIEW OF THE INVESTOR RELATIONS ART TODAY

Theodore H. Pincus
The Financial Relations Board

Lest anybody kid anybody, investor relations is by no means a science but an art. An immature one at that.

Indeed, over its past 40 years of recorded history, it has grown to be an expensive — and some say indispensable — part of 20th century corporate life. According to our annual survey, the 10,000 actively traded publicly held American companies will spend a record $5.4 billion on investor relations in 1988, as compared with an estimated $4 billion in 1986 and $2.9 billion in 1983.

But during much of that four-decade period of infancy and adolescence, the field's growth has been sorely retarded by ambiguity bred of its own self-consciousness. It didn't know exactly what it wanted to be when it grew up, and was guilt-stricken about stating its most obvious purpose.

From the beginning, of course, everyone agreed that investor relations was a corporate function different from advertising, public relations, treasury, legal affairs, or protocol. And yet it was expected to utilize some of the disciplines from each of these departments in helping the modern American company communicate more effectively with its own shareholders and the investment community at large.

But why? What was it all for?

In my view, investor relations has always had a four-tier objective:

- Legality.
- Credibility.
- Comfort.
- Stock support.

The first tier ensures that the public corporation maintains *legality* in its financial communications, that its flow of information observes all the rules set forth by law and subsequent SEC guidelines.

The second tier mandates that the company go beyond the minimum requirements and generate an atmosphere of *credibility* — one in which all information provided by the company can be trusted.

The third tier embraces a goal of creating genuine *comfort* among investors holding, or considering purchase of, the company's stock. This involves not merely generating trust but real understanding of the company's accounting practices, competitive position, industry outlook, strategic business plan, management performance standards and goals, and contingency scenarios.

The fourth and ultimate tier is tangible *stock support.* This goal involves the attainment of a climate that can produce a *maximum sustainable price/earnings ratio,* broad-scale expertise on the company's fundamentals among key investment professionals, consistent stock sponsorship, and strong liquidity of trading volume that can in turn offer stability in the marketplace.

However, even these nice things have not been ends in themselves. Combined with *staying power,* they set the stage for the true payoff: *more economical corporate growth.* This could be implemented by

- Improved ability to utilize common stock to raise further expansion capital.
- Improved ability to utilize common stock to pay for acquisitions.

- A more meaningful stock option program, to attract and retain key executive talent.
- Reduced vulnerability to hostile takeover attempts.

During a large part of its history, the investor relations field was often too timid to advance beyond tiers one and two. Brimming with altruism, IR practitioners piously proclaimed that their ultimate service to the corporation should be simply to achieve high standards of tier one or tier two — i.e., "Get the word out, and do it with credibility." In major segments of the field, this mentality thus brought about an evolution of the art focused primarily on *responsiveness*. Among corporations coast to coast, a frequent measurement of professional performance in IR was how adroitly the practitioner *responded* to outside stimuli: the inquiring investment analyst, the irate shareholder, the curious money manager, the nosy financial reporter.

Even now in the late 80s, much of the field is a quagmire of passive professionals, reacting with a doorman mentality to any interest volunteered. Like an immense investor information booth, IR rates its performance on the basis of how many of the curious go away satisfied and how few feathers are ruffled.

But it takes marketing savvy, ample energy, and a truly proactive posture in order to attain tier three and four of IR's overall objective. It takes resolve and a plan to seek out those elements of the investment community who can be *tomorrow's* supporters of the stock. Given the inherently fickle nature of the investor — amateur and professional — no company has ever consistently maintained an above-average multiple without working at it diligently every quarter to attract new blood and to create new experts in the stock.

If companies choose to make that commitment, can IR deliver? Is IR really capable of doing more than keeping people informed and happy? Does a marketing-oriented, proactive IR program have a measurable impact?

Throughout the 60s and 70s, skeptics abounded. They pointed cynically at the Efficient Market Theory propounded by University of Chicago scholars and others who loftily contended that the stock market always automatically discounts corporate fundamentals. Thus, they said, with virtually all public companies, all potential investors already understand all material changes in the fundamentals as they occur, and the price adjusts accordingly. No amount of good corporate communications can make a whit of difference.

But as the 80s arrived, American business history became so replete with case upon case utterly disproving Efficient Market punditry that even the pundits recanted one by one. As more and more companies demonstrated that they can indeed wake up the investor to an undervalued set of fundamentals and make a permanent difference in the PE multiple, skepticism waned rapidly.

Hence, many public companies across America have already learned the lesson and today are believers. More believers are created every week, as companies see IR become a results-driven, highly mobile weapon that can help accelerate the overall achievements of ambitious management teams. Increasingly, CEOs are recognizing that they are not hired to boost sales or even profits, but to make their shareholders rich. Plain and simple. "Enhancing shareholder value" has suddenly become a trendy buzz-phrase of the late 80s.

And yet many perceptive CEOs recognized this responsibility long ago, rolled up their sleeves, and set to work trying to broaden the base of their street support. They compared the modest amount of sweat and money required by proactive IR with the amount of sweat and money required to boost corporate sales, let's say, by 10 percent in order to attain a 10-percent gain in earnings — in order to reach (at a constant PE multiple) the same 10 percent gain in market value that might have accrued through intensified communications.

What are the primary tactics of proactive IR today? In our view, they are:

1. Adopting policies that can make the stock more marketable. This means that top management and directors will make a commitment to these principles:
   a. Establishing credibility must come before comfort.
   b. Information reduces risk. Management must share with investors its business plan, so that it can be evaluated.
   c. The smart strategy must always be to focus attention on *weaknesses* in company fundamentals. This is the grist

from whence upside potentials (sales growth, improved margins) can appear!

d. Proximity is the key. Out of sight, out of mind. The key communications job is to establish a personal bond, creating a flock of new scholars on the company story.

e. This is one job the CEO cannot delegate. The CEO must personify the company, articulate the story, and do so by taking it personally to the marketplace.

2. Effectively defining the company outlook and packaging a well-documented story for maximum comprehension; and then having the courage to update it continually as conditions change.

3. Upgrading the company's printed materials to focus on tomorrow.

4. Taking full advantage of high-tech hardware for broader reach: videotapes, video teleconferences, reports in disc form.

5. Aggressively working for in-depth, consistent treatment by the regional and national financial media.

6. Utilizing proven market research techniques in scouting the marketplace to identify the highest potential candidates for stock sponsorship — rather than wasting top management time in constant wild goose chases on the general forum luncheon circuit.

7. Utilizing top management time in a rationed, focused series of private group meetings through the year with prequalified, selected investment professionals.

8. Conducting a methodical follow-up program with every audience.

And how should all this be measured?

In our opinion, while IR will always remain an art, there is indeed a set of quasiscientific yardsticks by which any such corporate effort can and should be scored. They include:

- Depth interviews with financial professionals in debriefings, following CEO interviews.
- Surveys of attitudes among investment professionals following company contact — through direct personal interviews, never through mass mailings of questionnaires.

- Shareholder surveys.
- Debriefings with private group audiences within 48 hours of company meetings.
- Another follow-up with attendees, six weeks later.
- Measurements of the flow, strength, and accuracy of market letters.
- Index services such as Vickers and 13-4 filings with the SEC by institutional holders.
- Comparison of the stock trading volume with its own historic pattern, the market in general, and its stock group.
- Comparison of the aggregate change in market value with historical and industry patterns.
- The PE multiple.
- The price/book ratio.
- The ultimate test: company stock support in direct correlation to its stock group as reflected by *Media General Financial Weekly* and other sources.

WHAT KIND OF BUSINESS PLAN DO INVESTORS NEED?

It isn't vital that a corporate CEO get up on the soapbox and predict the company's earnings per share for next quarter or next year. As former head of Arthur Andersen (and strong proponent of public forecasts) Leonard Spacek once said: "The need of the long-term public investor is not the forecast of a single year...but a reliable basis on which to approximate growth over a period of at least several years...."

What today's investment professional needs most is the executive's willingness simply to share the valid ingredients of his own optimism — if indeed he is hopeful for profitable growth. And since the CEO alone is the architect of a corporate growth blueprint, he can best articulate the economic assumptions upon which it is based and the long-term objectives encompassed. Essentially, he must treat the investor audience as if it were a solitary individual who is considering buying the entire business outright. What would the buyer have to know? The key questions that must be answered are:

1. What is the company's true business mix?
   - What are the truly meaningful business segments?
   - Where are the assets?
   - Where are the earnings coming from?
   - Which segments are growing and which are flat?
   - Which segments have operating ratios superior to their industry norms?
   - What significant shifts have there been in the proportional relationship of these segments in the past three years?

2. What is the competitive position of each business segment in its respective market?
   - Which ones are low-cost producers?
   - What proprietary technological advantages are there?
   - What shifts have taken place in market share?
   - Do production locations offer advantages?
   - How about distribution?
   - How about marketing/advertising muscle?
   - What about financial resources compared with those of competitors?

3. What is the market outlook for each segment?
   - What worldwide or nationwide trends will influence generic product demand over the next five years?
   - What is a best-case scenario?
   - What is a worst-case scenario?

4. What are the company's basic weaknesses?
   - In what markets has the surface barely been scratched?
   - What profit drains are there and how can these be stemmed?
   - In what segments do operating ratios fall below industry norms, and what steps are being taken to improve these and widen margins?

5. What are management's goals and standards of performance?
   - What rates of return are the business fundamentals capable of attaining?
   - What is a best-case scenario?
   - What is a worst case scenario?
   - What are the underlying economic assumptions?
   - How may these expectations compare with the GNP and our industry averages?

6. What is management's strategy to achieve those goals?
   - How will the business mix be changed?
   - What product and marketing strategies will enhance the competitive position of each segment?
   - On what market opportunities can we capitalize by decisive action?
   - What will this plan cost, and where will the money come from?
   - What is the likely timetable?
   - What short-term sacrifices — if any — might be necessary to achieve this plan?
7. What is the company's "adaptability quotient"?
   - What is the company's built-in flexibility to meet changing external conditions?
   - If market demand exceeds our hopes and budgets, how quickly can we move to take maximum advantage of the potential extra revenues and profits that might be available?
   - If the worst-case scenario begins to emerge, how quickly can we retrench? How rapidly can we lower our break-even point, and what is our ability to weather a protracted storm?
   - How does all this apply to our physical plant?
   - How flexible is our work force?
   - How flexible are our loan agreements?
   - And finally, of utmost importance, how much will the factor of *financial leverage* play in the achievement of our ROE goal and the overall success of our Business Plan?

It is important to note that nowhere in this business plan requirement is there a necessity to render promises or issue absolute predictions. Nor is there the need to forecast next year's earnings per share. Indeed, what counts the most is that investors can acquire some confidence that management truly does have a game plan and is not merely sitting there waiting for the phone to ring. After learning the details of the game plan, investors can scrutinize it with care, appraise its wisdom, and evaluate the soundness of its assumptions and the likelihood of its success.

FIVE MYTHICAL REASONS TO KEEP ONE'S MOUTH SHUT

Long gone is any substance behind the myths that in the past have inhibited so many corporate CEOs, filled them with trepidation about "forecasting," and tied their tongues. For example: "If I talk about the future, am I not flirting with SEC problems?" No, not if the projections are made in good faith and based upon sound assumptions. In fact, the Securities & Exchange Commission has long condoned qualified projections that offer investors a glimpse of management's plans and expectations. Regulation S-K under the Securities Exchange Act of 1934 lays out quite palatable guidelines for the CEO. It states that "the Commission encourages the use of documents specified in Rule 175 under the Securities Act and Rule 3B-6 under the Exchange Act, of management's projections of future economic performance that have a reasonable basis and are presented in an appropriate format."

Another common myth is "If I talk about the future, won't the analysts think that I am touting the stock?" Hardly. Investment analysts almost always applaud those corporate managements enlightened enough to present a reasonable focus of their goals and strategies. Conversely, most companies that remain in the closet are today viewed as uncooperative and archaic — and quite often their stock sells at a penalty discount. Some of the most dignified, statesmanlike CEOs in the nation have been out there aggressively and consistently briefing investors on their plans, and in the process have been earning respect, not losing it.

Still another myth: "If I talk about the future, won't I give aid and comfort to the competition?" This one is fading fast, in an era when competitive intelligence is both widespread and easy to conduct. Most often, competitors are the first to know, not the last.

Many other CEOs plead, "If I talk about the future, what happens if I'm wrong?" Today, more than ever, sophisticated investors and professional analysts fully recognize that no corporate executive has a perfect crystal ball and that any projection is only a projection. That's why few of them swallow any business plan in its entirety as an absolute prediction of things to come. Instead, they are impressed that a plan indeed exists, impressed that it is founded upon a logical scenario, and impressed with the goals enunciated by management. Contrary to traditional corporate lore, hard-bitten investment professionals are rather *forgiving* when companies miss the mark and things don't turn out as painted in the original picture.

This is true *as long as one ingredient is present in the equation: Management's willingness to update the scenario as often as necessary.* In other words, under today's ground rules, it's virtually impossible to be called either a liar or a bum if you are able to communicate your dream effectively, and then promptly return to your audience with an updated version of that dream as circumstances force alterations upon you. In fact, if the ability to adapt to changing conditions is revered as a lofty attribute of champion executives, then your forced exercise of altering the business plan may well lend public testimony to the measure of your agility.

And finally, there's the cry: "My story isn't quite ready yet!" The funny thing about that apprehension is that, in 25 years, I've never known a CEO supremely confident that his story was totally *ready* to open on Broadway (much less Wall Street). By the nature of the beast, every CEO is forever agonizing over his game plan, constantly fiddling with his palette, touching up a few more specks on the canvas, reluctant to stand back, view the picture, and pronounce it complete. Nonetheless, he does have a plan, he is pursuing it, he does have goals and standards, the stock opens for trading every morning, and investors operating in an uncomfortable vacuum are either unduly bullish or unduly bearish.

HAS IT REALLY PAID OFF?

It is axiomatic that *information reduces risk,* and there are strong indications that this correlates with a sustainable enhancement of the price/earnings multiple.

In 1977 Pullman, Inc., was plagued with the same low price/earnings multiple as the other humdrum railroad equipment manufacturers with whom it was inextricably identified. In truth, however, CEO Sam Casey was hard at work yanking Pullman into the 20th century and moving it rapidly into a premier position as a provider of construction and engineering services — a far cry from the low-margin, highly cyclical railroad parts business. The problem was that few investors understood the business plan. When we interviewed him in depth, Larry Chaitt, a top analyst at The Bank of New York, observed:

"Pullman today is basically a multi-market company and the problem is that it is going to fall between the cracks as most institutions. You can describe the company in any one of a number of ways. As far as The Bank of New York is concerned, it falls in the rail equipment group. As far as the street perception of it, the earnings will fluctuate with freight car orders.... What management has to do is clean up their breakdowns and the cash flow statement, to give us some way of relating cash to earnings. They've got to be more willing to discuss those factors that affect Kellogg and Swindell, and the background of the industries they serve. They must explain their technology better. What factors in the world economy influence it? They've got to explain the economics of their business. They are an international company. The interrelationships between Pullman and some of the factors that affect the world market are important. This is a stock that I like. It's one that I follow and one that I'll continue to follow. However, I've got other projects that I think are more pressing. I've got no time for Pullman...."

At the same time, Robert Dunlap, a top analyst at the Irving Trust Co., said:

"I don't follow Pullman because they won't tell you enough about their business to let you get a handle on it. I've looked at Pullman in the past, and I've called on the company about three times. I've always had an open mind toward the company, especially when the stock is cheap like this.... I think it would be very helpful if management had periodic meetings with the street, but when they do so, they have to give the facts. Their annual and quarterly reports are not good. They need to be broken down. If they change and become more open with the street, there is no doubt that I'd take more of an interest in Pullman. The key thing is disclosing what is going on, which will take care of 85% of their problems."

Sam Casey decided to change things. He decided it was time for the broad-range investors to understand that Pullman was a new company, a business in which the *service* sector was quickly emerging as the dominant profit maker. An effort was launched to have Pullman completely recategorized in the eyes of the investment community as a purveyor of services. The market outlook and competitive position — especially for Pullman's growing construction and engineering services — were clearly delineated through all communications channels. Sam Casey personally led the effort with forays throughout the investment community to explain his aspirations and strategies. And, in an effort to dramatize the point, Pullman asked *Fortune Magazine* to "delist" it from the Fortune 500, which are industrial companies, and spotlight the fact that Pullman should rightly be classified as a *services* company.

In the years that followed, the message increasingly hit home. In many securities firms, the task of following Pullman stock was shifted from the rail equipment analysts to the analysts following services companies, most of which carried substantially higher PE multiples. And, despite a series of setbacks that included a major New York subway contract cost overrun and other problems, Pullman picked up broad new investor support. By 1980, its PE multiple had moved from 8X to 11X, and its total market value had moved from $338 million to $524 million.

In late 1978, Chicago-based Jewel Companies, Inc., with a PE multiple of 6X, was languishing in a stock market quagmire along with most of its brethren classified as grocery store chains. Even Jewel's modern management techniques and aggressive leadership in supermarketing could not convince investors that Jewel deserved a superior rating. The popular perception was of a bright company stuck in a dull industry. When she was interviewed at the time, Priscilla Perry, a senior analyst at Chicago Title and Trust, emphasized that, "the long term industry outlook for retail food stores is bleak...the industry is very mature...the industry and the investment community have overplayed the benefits of inflation and are fooling themselves in considering inflation a positive factor."

Ted Breckel, a highly respected analyst at The Northern Trust, added that, "the industry has below average appeal...

Jewel's major market share in Chicago is probably their biggest strength. Their most glaring weakness is the inability to grow in non-food merchandising." Meanwhile, Charles Wetzel, a top retail trade analyst at Citibank, New York, pointed out that "it would help their image somewhat if they were involved more in the drug area."

In reality, Jewel's very enlightened management team, led by Don Perkins and Wes Christopherson, had *big plans* to change the company's fundamental business mix and was making decisive moves to broaden the company's base. Jewel wasn't there yet, but it was aspiring to become a major *diversified retailer* rather than merely a supermarket chain. One key to this effort was a massive program to expand Jewel's Osco Drug Division. But how could Jewel adjust investor perception to keep pace with — or move somewhat ahead of — its accomplishments?

Essentially, Jewel's answer was to draft a growth manifesto — a business plan put on paper in the form of a detailed corporate profile and also packaged for presentation to live audiences and media in a conservative, orderly sequence of events. This sequence unfolded methodically throughout 1979, 1980, 1981, and thereafter. In its corporate profile Jewel went to great lengths to put real substance behind its announced aspirations The summary section of one profile said, "Although Jewel will continue to be a major food retailer, its strategic plans call for reduced reliance on the traditional supermarket format. Future plans put major emphasis on expansion of the company's 117 combination food/drug stores and its 286 solo drug stores. By 1985, the company expects that 85% of its U.S. earnings will be contributed by combination stores, side by side units, and stand alone drug stores."

Jewel then provided documentation to underscore both the seriousness and aggressiveness of its business plan. This data included actual projections of supermarkets, drug stores, discount grocery stores, and convenience stores showing 1982 actual and projected figures for 1983, 1984, and 1985, in both number of units and total square feet of retail space.

Increasingly, the message hit home, especially as Jewel's management articulated the story personally to assembled groups of institutional money managers and retail brokerage executives through an extensive series of private group meetings conveniently tied to normal routine business trips. By June 1984, the company's PE multiple had advanced from 6X to 9X, and its total market value had increased from $220 million to $649 million.

AFG Industries in 1980 was a small company in the town of Kingsport, in the hills of Eastern Tennessee, run by a colorful, enterprising young CEO named Dee Hubbard. Hubbard was trying to build a name and position for the struggling company in the nation's glass industry. Rather than go up against the well-known giants in markets across the board, the company selected several attractive segments of the specialty glass market, such as the types used in solar heating and other specialized areas, and also applied new advanced technologies to the traditional processes of producing glass. Hubbard had a game plan incorporating these new technologies, including several expansion moves — both internal and external — that could propel his company into position as the third or fourth largest glass producer in the United States within the following few years.

Dee Hubbard chose to share his plans with stockholders and the investment community. Obviously, there were many aspects of his strategy that could not be divulged for competitive reasons, but the overall goals and aims of the company were laid out in its 1981 annual report and the intensive communications program that followed.

AFG consistently updated its published strategy each step of the way and kept investors closely advised as to adjustments and modifications as the company adapted to changing circumstances in the glass industry. Overall, the scenario developed quite close to original plan and the company's sales and profits grew rapidly.

From the outset of the program effort in May 1980, when the company had a total market value of $15 million and a PE multiple of only 3.7X, AFG won an increasingly wider scope of recognition, and by December 1982 — just two years later — found itself in an enviable position with which to capitalize on its equity leverage. Its market value had risen tenfold to $174 million, and its PE multiple had risen to 15X. At that point AFG elected to bring to market an additional 750,000 shares of common stock, raising $14.8 million, $10 million more than what would have been raised under circumstances existing just two years earlier.

By 1987, AFG Industries was on the NYSE with a market value advanced to $650 million. Further, it had an extremely active following by top glass industry analysts and special situations analysts coast to coast, plus a number of top money managers in major institutions.

WHAT HAPPENS IF WE STUMBLE?

The stock market lives on expectation. When a revised set of expectations is not as bright as the originally published set of expectations, investors react. The stock goes down.

But one difference notable among most companies that have seen fit to make public projections is that frequent updating of those projections can provide a *soft letdown,* rather than a hard landing, in terms of investor response. In other words, companies that refuse to discuss expectations must simply issue press releases many weeks after the end of each quarter presenting the final figures for that period and let the stock react as it may. Conversely, those that provide frequent updating of anticipated results extend an early warning system to the Street and, if the factors behind the figures can be adequately understood, a soft landing can result.

WHY GET INVOLVED AT ALL?

Even if the open-door policy is truly effective in creating the climate for a maximum sustainable PE multiple, is it worth the effort? Is it worth establishing a new modus vivendi with the Street, the inevitable, ongoing dialogue, and lingering anxiety over one's personal credibility? Most assuredly there is no automatic answer for every company. While uncertainty is a basic fact of life in virtually any business, some businesses — during various stages of their lives — face uncertainties too incalculable to manage in public. These are factors that any responsible businessperson must weigh.

Nonetheless, I believe that for a wide range of publicly held U.S. companies business conditions in the nineties will present several compelling reasons why a more open policy should be seriously considered.

First, although the capital markets have been awash with easy money, many economists are pointing to a significant tightening of the market for borrowed funds in the early years of the next decade. When this is combined with an already widening debt/equity ratio trend among public companies, it seems obvious that competition for equity capital will intensify. *Accordingly, the difference of even one multiple point in a company's stock value may make the difference in its ability to continue growth on an economical basis by raising expansion capital.* Meanwhile, in the face of this, the stock market seems to be no less inefficient than it ever was. Even among the academic cognoscenti who were the prime proponents of modern portfolio theory, there has been a major shift in thinking. In fact, in 1985 cult father Barr Rosenberg acknowledged in the *Journal of Portfolio Management* that he had come to the "inescapable conclusion that prices of the New York Stock Exchange are inefficient."

Second, growth by acquisition should be a continuing option for many corporate boards. The pattern is too clear to ignore: a corporate landscape littered with cases where companies — correctly valued by the marketplace — capitalize further on that good fortune by trading stock for the shares of companies that are undervalued.

Third, most pundits see no end to the stream of hostile takeovers in the years ahead, despite innovative legal maneuverings that pop up each year. Every ingenious defense has inspired an equally ingenious offense, yet no attorney in the nation has ever acknowledged the existence of an antitakeover posture that is better than a strong, well-valued stock price.

Last, there is the question of CEO responsibility. If the inherent inefficiencies of the marketplace prevent adequate recognition of his company's underlying values and potentials, who will help the market correct itself? If the CEO refuses to share his vision of tomorrow, sticks purely to his knitting, and insists that the record stand on its own, can the market rely on anything but yesterday? If so, shareholders may indeed have to wait long beyond tomorrow for any reasonable dimension of reward — and between now and then may well ask why.

* * * * *

Theodore H. Pincus is chairman, managing partner, and majority owner of The Financial Relations Board, the nation's largest Investor Relations agency, according to Fortune magazine and the O'Dwyer Directory. Over his 30-year career he has counseled more than 300 publicly held corporations and has earned more than 50 national and regional awards for professional excellence, including The Silver Anvil for investor relations, the industry's highest award.

ESTABLISHING THE INVESTOR RELATIONS FUNCTION

Johnnie Johnson
Georgeson & Company, Inc.

At most publicly held companies, the investor relations (IR) function has been structured through an evolutionary process. As a result, most of these companies are essentially organized by default. The varied ways in which a company interacts with investors have developed piecemeal over decades. The responsibility for each piece of the IR puzzle generally was assigned to the functional area most conversant with the technical aspects of filling that specific need as it arose. Accordingly, in most companies the only true IR executive is the CEO. No other executive within the corporate structure has the responsibility of coordinating and directing the full spectrum of relationships linking the company and its investors.

At best, this ad hoc approach works only adequately. At worst, it fails under stress. Many would argue that the ultimate oversight of IR is clearly every CEO's responsibility and unquestioned prerogative. Indeed, CEO-as-senior-IR-officer is one of many effective approaches to structuring IR. As we will see, there is no single "magic" structure for the function.

There is, however, a vast difference between the ad hoc lumping of the varied aspects of IR under the CEO as opposed to the thoughtful coordination of these functions under the chief executive. The second approach takes into account the components of IR, how these elements interact, and the experience, perspective, and team orientation of the parties involved. In short, it m*anages* the structure instead of reacting to external stimuli piecemeal.

Even when ad hoc IR is functional, the unfortunate fact is that "adequate" is not equivalent to "good." Ad hoc IR usually leaves shareholder dollars on the table. Ultimately, this puts stress on the corporation. A break-up artist can be attracted to undervalued shares. Analysts and brokers can become exasperated with disjointed and unfocused corporate information and abandon the stock. The company's stock price can fall farther than that of its industry peers in bad times and rise less in good times, eroding investor confidence. Under such stress, the cracks in an ad hoc IR structure become chasms precisely when the board and CEO have the least available time and energy to repair them.

In this chapter, we will:

- Review some real-world examples of ad hoc IR and resulting failures.
- Define IR as an integrated marketing function.
- Examine the basic subfunctions that collectively fall within the purview of IR.
- Prescribe an approach to establishing IR's charter, structure, and resources to enhance the scope of its contribution to shareholder value day to day, while insulating it from structural failure under stress.

IN HINDSIGHT, I GUESS WE SHOULD'VE DONE IT DIFFERENTLY

To my mind, nothing better identifies potential problems than case histories of failure. The ones that follow are fictionalized, and each melds together elements from two or three actual companies. This has not been done to protect the guilty.

Rather, it has been done to present the typical. Let me stress that the real-world models for the following minicases are generally well-managed companies. Because of the pervasive nature of ad hoc IR in the corporate universe, the only difference between them and scores of peer companies is circumstance, not fundamental business competence.

The Case of the "Safe" IR Campaign

Universal Utilities was caught in a regulatory bind between customers and suppliers. Future earnings were in doubt. Predictably, the stock price dropped. Even though the company successfully began to unwind itself from miles of red tape, the price didn't recover. Universal's communications, legal, and investor relations departments had a long history of turf conflict, it seems. Because of the resulting paralysis, no coordinated attempt was made to communicate how the firm was solving its problems. In fact, Universal's most visible communications effort was a multimillion-dollar "feel-good" advertising campaign associating its name with successful celebrities. The ads said virtually nothing about the company, its operations, or its financial condition — a truly "safe" communications strategy in a period of uncertainty. The ads generated hundreds of complimentary letters and requests for reprints, convincing the CEO that the campaign was effective. However, without a concise, coordinated presentation of how the company's strategies were building value, investors didn't turn these good feelings into a higher stock price. Ultimately, an attack by a corporate raider tipped off Wall Street to Universal's hidden values. The company escaped only by literally giving away one of its most valuable subsidiaries.

The Case of the Two-Faced Turnaround

Wholesale Widgets, Inc., was emerging from a competitive firestorm. Computerized, decentralized distributors with cheap, Asian sources of widgets had nearly buried the old-line, fully integrated widget supplier. Market share slumped and cash flow wilted, while write-downs and debt soared. Chairman/CEO/

President/COO Aldon Brown sold assets, shut down antiquated production facilities, slashed staff, rebuilt his distribution system into a state-of-the-art wonder, and assembled a global stable of low-cost suppliers in just 18 months. Consumed with operations and restructuring, Brown turned day-to-day communications over to two aggressive executives who had replaced early retirees. IR and shareholder services went to a new corporate secretary and chief legal counsel, while PR and advertising went to a new CFO. Each was given the same charge: "Handle it. I want solutions, not problems." The CFO presided over all press interviews, stressing cash flow to reassure lenders. At his direction, oversize, four-color financial graphs dominated the annual report. On the other hand, the firm's businesses were represented by table-top photos of product lines accompanied by dry text that reviewed business segments. Under the guidance chief legal counsel, in an effort to maintain "credibility," securities analyst contacts, 10-Ks, and 10-Qs stressed the competitive pressures and financial constraints that continued to face the company. Furthermore, PR and IR staff saw the text of each others' efforts for the first time only on publication, even though preliminary drafts were routinely circulated to their respective corporate officers. Nowhere were Brown's overall goals, his strategy for obtaining them, or a report card on implementation presented. Even though Widget had clearly succeeded in revitalizing its business, its stock price and key ratios routinely continued to lag far behind those of peers.

The Case of the "Slam-Dunk" Proxy Vote

Ace Manufacturing CEO John Smith felt an integrated, professional IR effort was not needed. In fact, the company was proud of its "open door/open phone" policy for investors. Shareholders or analysts could call Ace's CEO or CFO directly. One day, Smith noted that many of his peers were instituting classified boards of directors — i.e., only one third or one fourth of their directors were elected in any given year. He asked Ace's counsel how shareholder approval fared for such boards. A brief review showed that the vast majority passed. Convinced approval was a "slam dunk," Ace put a classified board proposal on its next annual meeting proxy, unaware that many institutional stockholders vote against such proposals as a matter of policy, viewing them as "antitakeover" devices. Since nearly 70 percent of Ace's stock was held by institutions, the proposal was a sure loser. Most companies perform a vote projection based on their particular stockholder base before deciding to submit a controversial proposal to shareholders. Those proposals with any significant chance of losing are seldom put to a vote, which is why history shows unrealistically high success rates for such proposals. Smith learned this only after withdrawing his proposal just before Ace's annual meeting to avoid the embarrassment of public defeat. In addition, Smith inadvertently branded himself as "entrenchment-oriented" in the minds of several of his largest stockholders. Smith made one of IR's most common mistakes. He thought in terms of "the market," rather than h*is* market.

Common to all these cases of structural failure is an absence of coordination and cooperation. In my experience, this virtually always stems from the lack of a shared sense of overall purpose among the various subdisciplines of the IR function. Without an umbrella concept of the total function, each subgroup develops its own, often unstated, sense of mission based on its own technical capabilities and view of the world.

The inevitable compromises and risk/reward decisions each group must accommodate as it interacts with the others then degenerate into defense of the one true faith from the misguided. Attorneys protect the company from glitzy PR types, who protect it from clubbish IR types, who protect it from myopic accountants, who protect it from an overenthusiastic CEO, who protects it from nitpicking attorneys, ad infinitum. Mix this with corporate stress and the normal, healthy competition that routinely exists among senior managers, and these conflicts escalate from guerilla skirmishes into intractable turf wars.

The central irony is that each player genuinely feels that his or her group, and that group alone, truly understands corporate needs. All too often, the CEO has no integrated view of the IR function. As a result, the CEO acts as referee, rather than as coach or team manager.

WHAT'S THIS THING WE CALL "THE MARKET"?

The goal of IR can be stated simply. It is to generate *fair market value* for a company's securities. It is a marketing function in the fullest sense of the term.

The fact that the securities market in large part is channeled through auction-style exchanges similar to the commodities markets obscures the actual dynamics of securities valuation. To be sure, the commodities model has its uses, especially in interpreting short-term price moves in a single stock. However, commodities are fungible — i.e., one bushel of corn is interchangeable with any other of the same type and grade regardless of where it was grown — while stocks are not. A $1,000 investment in Ford, for example, is no more interchangeable with a $1,000 investment in General Motors than a Thunderbird is interchangeable with a Corvette.

Ultimately, the value of a security rests on what buyers and sellers believe, accurately or not, about who issued the security, the issuers' track record, and the characteristics of the security itself. These are some of the key factors used to value a specific security in relation to the investor's overall set of beliefs about the firm's industry and the general economy; in contrast, with a true commodity only industry and economic factors need be considered.

In addition, although the New York, American, and NASDAQ exchanges appear to create central markets that directly bring together buyer and seller, the pathways through which these transactions truly occur usually resemble spilled spaghetti. Furthermore, new securities hit the market almost daily, while old ones disappear into mergers, LBOs, and bankruptcies. Such a complex market, with its constantly changing product offerings, more closely resembles the market for automobiles than for pork bellies.

Clearly, talking about "The market" as if it were similar to commodities trading is to engage in gross oversimplification. "The market" is extraordinarily segmented in terms of buyer/seller characteristics. Securities are equally variegated. Further, "fair" and "value" are at root subjective terms whose combined meaning may well be as discretely individual to each and every investor as a fingerprint.

However, the same dynamics can be said to apply to any widely traded manufactured product. For the majority of the goods we buy, competing producers and product variations constantly proliferate. In reality, "channels" of distribution more resemble a street map of Los Angeles than the clean flowcharts found in business texts. Product information assails us from all sides. As consumers of products, each of us routinely participates in markets as complex, convoluted, and subjective as "the market." Indeed, the management discipline we call "marketing" evolved precisely because producers and distributors needed to systematically deal with the complex market systems that have developed in our industrial economies.

For exactly the same reasons, defining IR as a marketing function can make the complexity of the securities markets manageable. It allows us to identify those forces we can legitimately affect, and those to which we must adjust. It allows us to sort out which aspects of each IR subdiscipline are technical, which are tactical, and which are strategic. As a result, it allows us to focus and direct our efforts toward a common end: fair market value.

WHY ARE STOCKS AND BONDS LIKE CARS AND TRUCKS?

As you can see, I like to use the automotive industry to illustrate how closely IR resembles the marketing of manufactured products. It doesn't stretch the imagination to view an investment as a durable product, similar to a car or truck.

In both cases, fashion has much to do with selection. After a while, each is usually traded in for a new model. Fashion may have changed, customer needs may have changed, or the product may have been found disappointing. Every now and then, the customer keeps the product until it wears out. Except for debt securities, with investments this is seldom by choice. With both types of purchase, there is a vast difference between what the product is and what most customers *buy*. For example, a car or truck is actually a complicated collection of metal, glass, ceramic, and plastic parts, with, occasionally, wood and leather trim. However, save for a handful of collectors, car and truck customers are not buying industrial sculpture, they are buying the discretionary freedom to move people and things.

Similarly, a security is an ownership claim on some portion of a business. This is true whether the security represents equity (a more or less permanent claim), debt (a claim that disappears when the debt is satisfied), or a hybrid (such as redeemable preferred stock). The vast majority of investors, however, are buying future financial returns, a very flexible form of discretionary freedom. In the case of both securities and vehicles, buyers choose among competing products based on the combination of fashion, comfort, speed, safety, and capacity they desire and can afford.

Both types of purchase involve retail sales and "fleet" or institutional sales. Both are affected by the opinions of brokers, consultants, media experts, and consumer advocates. Both face complex federal, state, and local regulation on product design and promotion.

In both instances, the buyer seldom focuses on what he or she actually owns unless the purchase has proved disappointing. The remedies available in both cases are quite similar. Sell the "lemon" to an unsuspecting buyer (the "greater fool" syndrome and typical first resort). Seek legal redress (start or join a class action suit). Insist the producer fix it (start or join a proxy fight). Fix it yourself (start a takeover). Get someone else to fix it (encourage a takeover). Junk it, and learn from the experience (a last resort that may sour the buyer forever on the product and its producer).

Naturally, in any customer/producer relationship, some dissatisfaction will always exist. Clearly, when widespread and uncorrected, such dissatisfaction is fatal to managements and often fatal to the firm itself, a fact of life supported amply by the experience of the U.S. auto industry over the past two decades. Indeed, in the case of securities, when the buyer can't bail out at a decent price, the first thing he or she focuses on is the real power over management embodied in ownership.

To be sure, these facts of corporate life are not lost on chief executives. It is rare indeed to find a CEO who will not readily acknowledge that a strong, mutually supportive relationship with both customers and owners is critical to the continued existence of any corporation. What is puzzling at most corporations is the yawning gap between their sophisticated approach to customer relations (i.e., product marketing) and their ad hoc approach to IR.

REPEAT AFTER ME: "IR IS A MARKETING FUNCTION"

Let's briefly review the basics of product marketing. The central element in any marketing program is market segmentation — breaking down the global market for any given product type into manageable chunks. Then specific products can be matched with the customer group or groups most likely to value them for the benefits they truly offer.

For each product, existing market segments are targeted for maintenance, growth, or exit. Prospective market segments are targeted for penetration. In each case, matching specific product benefits with market needs and desires informs the targeting process.

The segmentation and targeting process is central to the gathering of customer information, product development, promotion, advertising, press strategies, and so on. A clear understanding of the target groups, their motivations, and the need/benefit match are shared by all concerned. As the marketing cycle progresses, data on customer reaction, sales volumes, pricing trends, competitive moves, economic factors, and "fashion" trends feeds back into the system to guide adjustments in product design, packaging, promotion, targets, etc. — in essence creating a self-correcting, dynamic, team effort.

Throughout this process, legal and technical support is critical. Product claims must be technically justified and legally defensible. At the same time, they must be understandable by and appealing to the target customers. This is a delicate task, full of potential conflict. But, in product marketing, the players usually understand the trade-offs involved. Attorneys realize that an ad or a product brochure is useless if it can be understood only by other attorneys, or if it is so sanitized as to claim no benefits whatsoever for the buyer. Engineers understand that the customers' concept of value must take precedence over their knowledge of design. And, the promotional staff understands that sizzling sales material is ultimately harmful if it generates product liability suits or unrealistic customer expectations.

Unfortunately, this integrated marketing approach is virtually absent from most IR functions. For example, while most IR teams have one or two people who are fairly knowledgeable about the complexities of the securities markets, I would be truly surprised if the view of securities market segmentation generally shared throughout the function went much beyond the following two basic points:

1. Some investors are primarily yield-oriented; some are primarily growth-oriented; some seek a balance of each in the same security. (This is similar to saying some people buy cars, some buy trucks, and some buy station wagons.)
2. "The market" is divided between institutions and individuals. (This is the equivalent of saying vehicles are generally purchased by either businesses or households.)

In fact, I would wager that at many companies key people in corporate advertising, corporate press relations, and the corporate secretary's office couldn't be this specific in segmenting the securities markets.

Further, most publicly held companies don't even have a clear picture of their current shareholder population. Granted, assembling this information and keeping it current is a formidable task for some companies. For most, however, senior management would be surprised at the amount of usable market information that could be assembled in house if the task were approached by the whole IR team on an integrated basis.

Unfortunately, with only a vague picture of current shareholders and a sketchy view of the specific market segments for their securities, few corporations have a real IR marketing plan with measurable, clearly identified targets.

Without a common sense of mission throughout the corporation, ad hoc IR reigns supreme. The irony of this situation is that most companies already have in place the talent and reources to do first-rate IR marketing.

BEING HITCHED TOGETHER IS WHAT CREATES A TEAM

Although IR occupies its own little niche in the organizational chart below, the bulleted functions represent the *minimum* set of activities that actually comprise the IR function. Our chart simply recognizes that, in most corporations, the person or

Typical Organization of Shareholder Relations

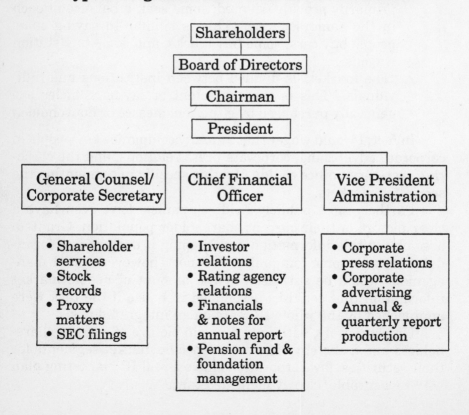

persons who carry the IR title seldom have direct responsibility for the full function. The fact is, anyone involved in executing any of these listed subfunctions is truly a member of a corporation's IR team, whether or not it is in his or her title or job description.

The particular organization and reporting structure shown is neither "right" nor "wrong." It is merely typical. Such a structure can function superbly or miserably, depending on the teamwork and common sense of mission that actually exists among the individuals involved.

In addition to the listed functions, there are three additional sources of potential full-time or part-time IR team members:

1. Corporate strategic planning.
2. Other communications/public affairs functions, such as speech writing, community relations, employee communications, and government relations.
3. Specialized outside counseling or consulting firms that support the IR subfunctions.

Let's review each group of functions in our chart in terms of basic duties, technical orientation (a source of both strength and weakness in an ad hoc IR environment), and the potential, often overlooked, contributions to a marketing-oriented IR team. We'll take them left to right as they appear on our chart. In the corporate world, the members of these groups often jokingly call themselves Legal Eagles, Bean Counters, and Image Merchants.

The Legal Eagles

Our first group of shareholder-related functions normally falls under a company's general counsel/corporate secretary because their technical execution has primarily legal ramifications.

Mistakes in shareholder services or stock records can seriously affect shareholder tax status, right to securities ownership, and right to vote on corporate matters. As a result, this function must be extremely accurate as it processes enormous amounts of detailed information.

Unfortunately, shareholder service/stock record functions are notoriously understaffed. Faced with mountains of critical detail work, these departments seldom have time to sit back and analyze the company's current investor population. Very little demographic analysis is done at this level so long as a company is not the subject of a proxy fight or a tender offer. Should one arise, tens of thousands of dollars are spent in a couple of weeks to have outside firms develop some of the insights into shareholder composition that could have been available all along from this group.

The irony here is that, properly executed and maintained, ongoing analysis of current investor demographics is a company's single most powerful source of information on market segmentation. In addition, ongoing investor demographics provide a report card on a company's IR program. But most companies review investor demographics on an ad hoc basis and seldom seek active participation by the very people who maintain shareholder records.

Similarly, proxy material and other SEC filings must conform not only to stringent and complex legislative and regulatory rules, but to numerous unwritten, but critical, quasilegal conventions as well.

A primary responsibility of attorneys is to keep their clients out of court. As a result, attorneys tend to be extremely risk averse. They tend to prefer the omission of information not required by law, or terse, general statements if there is any risk whatsoever of drawing SEC scrutiny or of laying a foundation for a future shareholder suit from professional "strike suit" investors.

In addition, attorneys are trained to use a form of legal English that, when properly executed, will be technically specific and unambiguous when read by a judge or fellow attorney. Terms are defined in excruciating detail and attached to shorthand labels that are then undeviatingly used in quotes throughout the legal document (i.e., "The Company," "The Merger"). Indeed, many a publicist has been called in to draft a press release to announce the spin-off of a corporate subsidiary with a legal name like "The Acme Screen Door Production and Unscheduled Airline Master Limited Partnership." This name is stated once in legal documents, and a tag, such as "Acme Partners," is used from there on for convenience.

Unfortunately, what may work in a prospectus often looks downright silly in a one-page news release. The fact is, few shareholders or business reporters are legally trained. As a result, when they attempt to read most SEC documents, their eyes glaze over at best, and they may well reach dangerously wrong conclusions if they attempt to interpret the complex syntax and obscure jargon with which many are laden.

As a practical matter, at most companies senior SEC counsel and communications specialists do establish a working relationship that permits some readability to be inserted into SEC documents. Typically, however, this happens late in the game, and the fixes tend to be more cosmetic than fundamental. Often, plain English explanations of complex transactions are restricted to oral presentations in "road shows" and in phone conversations with interested investors. They are not permitted to be broadly distributed in print.

The irony here is that the professional investor who has access to legal staff or has trained himself or herself in SEC jargon has the edge. This is, of course, precisely the opposite of what is sought by the SEC. A second irony is that the logical skills acquired by most attorneys can be invaluable in helping a communications specialist demystify complex corporate transactions for the general reader. However, this happens only when they bring their talents together early in the development of the document, and when they both share the same communications objective.

In summary:

• An integrated, market-driven IR program encourages shareholder service/stock records personnel to view their jobs as providing both service to the investor *and* valuable demographic feedback to the rest of the IR team.
• Similarly, such a program encourages the legal staff and communications specialists to (a) have a common goal, (b) appreciate and use each other's technical strengths, and (c) work together as early as possible to draft understandable, accurate, legally sound investor communications.

The Bean Counters

The group of subfunctions listed under the chief financial officer are usually placed there because each requires significant technical skill in financial analysis as well as familiarity with accepted accounting practices and conventions.

It is not at all unusual to find a "manager" or "director" of "investor relations" on the CFO's team. In recent years, this function has fundamentally changed in response to the institutionalization of Wall Street. One of this position's major responsibilities is providing securities analysts and portfolio managers a view into the detailed accounting practices that underlie a company's financial statements. This permits professional investors and investment advisors to more accurately build computerized financial models of the company.

To maintain the relationship, this function then provides the professionals with ongoing operating data (prices, volumes, market share, etc.) on lines of business, as well as insight into each business's dynamics. (Does cold weather help or hurt sales? What is the effect of high oil prices?) The objective is to (a) help the professional build a reasonably accurate and up-to-date model and (b) use that ongoing relationship to send strategic messages into the investment community. Interestingly, although many IR management slots originally were created to answer questions from individual investors, as a practical matter this individual is a small part of the function these days.

Given this heavy orientation toward operating numbers, it's not surprising that people in these slots often are recruited from the controller's office. Whether or not they have much of an involvement in annual and quarterly reports, analysts' speeches, corporate ads, press relations, or road shows designed to drum up investor interest depends largely on their personalities and the amount of turf warfare in their organizations. It is indeed rare for this style IR manager to have executive responsibility for much more than the day-to-day care and feeding of Wall Street's lions.

Next on our financial list is rating agency relations. Publicly traded debt securities are routinely given credit ratings by agencies such as Moody's and Standard & Poors. The issuing company meets with executives of these agencies on a regular basis, reporting to them on critical issues such as projected cash flow, coverage ratios, and implications of strategic plans, all as they affect a company's ability to service its debt. Major corporate moves, such as spin-offs, mergers, and large acquisitions, usually require special meetings to update agencies regarding debt-oriented implications of the transactions. These presentations often contain projections that are clearly nonpublic material information. Technically, the presentations are viewed as totally confidential, and in no way designed to sell, or offer to sell, securities.

Usually, dealing with rating agencies is the purview of the treasurer's department, although in most firms, the CFO takes the lead in major presentations and the CEO occasionally participates, as well. In fact, such relations are a critical element in IR for two reasons.

First, investors who hold debt securities are extremely important to any firm. In tough financial times, companies quickly realize that debt holders come before preferred or common stockholders. Recapitalizations normally require debt holders consent. And, in a worst case scenario of bankruptcy, debt holders call the shots.

Second, a positive or negative change in the ratings for a company's debt securities can often have a direct and immediate effect on the market price of its other securities — common and preferred stock.

Given the importance of debt securities, it is astounding that few companies truly integrate debt-holder and rating-agency relations into their overall IR activities. Not only are a firm's IR and corporate communications professionals often excluded from the preparation of such presentations, in some companies they never see the finished product. In fact, in a few, IR and communications staff are totally unaware such activities exist. Such a circumstance is potentially dangerous. For most firms, there is a natural tension between debt holders and equity holders.

Debt holders look for sufficient assets to cover the principal of their loans in the event of a liquidation, as well as assurances that the firm will generate more than enough free cash flow over the term of the bond or debenture to render the potential for liquidation virtually nil. In essence, they want to be like an insurance company providing fire coverage on an inventory of pig iron stored at the bottom of a lake. As their feelings of security decline, the interest rates they charge for their money rise exponentially.

On the other hand, in growth companies, equity holders want management to use the leverage provided by debt for investments that promise to generate superior growth in both book value and book earnings. Such investments are inherently risky. In fact, as the potential for such growth rises, risk normally rises even faster.

Further, in recent years activist investors have forced low-growth/high-cash-flow firms to load up on debt. In most of these cases, the borrowed cash was not for investment, but for direct distribution to shareholders. Regardless, substantially increased leverage means substantially increased risk. This is why much of the debt has been in the form of high-interest "junk bonds."

As you can see, financial communications can be quite a balancing act for many firms, requiring that the firms continuously interweave messages regarding financial strength and stability (for creditors) with information highlighting growth and earnings opportunities (for stockholders).

Whether corporations like it or not, debt holders read the same financial publications as equity holders. Should the messages they see there be at odds with those they wish to hear, or may be receiving directly from company officials, their feelings of comfort fall rapidly. The tight-wire act some firms must perform in balancing messages between debt and equity holders is performed in public. Not requiring those inside the company to coordinate both sets of messages is both dangerous and foolish. And yet, few firms officially make debt-holder relations a full-time part of IR.

Next on our list is the preparation of the financial statements and notes thereto that are an integral part of quarterly and annual reports to shareholders, as well as such major SEC documents as 10-Ks, 10-Qs, and prospectuses. These reports are prepared by, or under the direction of, professional accountants, most of whom are CPAs. Like attorneys, they work within a large body of intricate rules called *generally acceptable accounting principles,* or GAAP. Again, as in law, these rules allow for a great deal of flexibility. Depending on the particular theory applied, the same sets of business transactions can generate strikingly different financial statements. By and large, the notes to these statements are designed to alert the reader as to the particular approach being taken in each individual report.

Again, as with legal matters, the latitude this system allows can be misused. Most of the time, however, it simply provides a firm enough flexibility to present its business, which is unique, in a financial form relatively comparable to that of other firms, especially those in the same general line of business. In addition, the way various transactions are presented can have large tax consequences for both the firm and its securities holders. Therefore, thinking through the best way to structure a transaction for tax purposes is an important task for most financial departments.

Investor relations problems often arise when those in the accounting function becomes so involved in this complex process that they temporarily lose sight of the fact that they are charged with providing the owners of the company an intelligible financial report on the progress of the firm. While the statement and notes may make sense to another accountant, in many cases, they may as well be written in Russian as far as most investors are concerned.

Unfortunately, the communications professionals in most companies are simply handed completed financial statements and notes, including the critical MD & A (Management's Discussion and Analysis of Financial Condition and Operating Results) that are required for most SEC and shareholder reports. They have little input in forming these documents, are seldom encouraged to critique them, and, in most cases, have not been trained to truly understand them. As a result, the communication professionals have little opportunity to help demystify the more arcane sections of a company's financials.

When given the opportunity and training, communication experts can be quite helpful. For example, one oil and gas company I know of had to write off an investment of more than $100 million in an exploratory well. As initially prepared, the company's funds flow statement did not adjust "cash flow provided by operations" to reflect the fact that 95 percent of the investment had been made in prior years. That adjustment was made elsewhere in the funds flow statement, and comments in the notes made the facts clear to any trained accountant. How-

ever, to the average reader, it appeared that the entire investment had been made in the current quarter, and that this dry
hole had soaked up nearly half of the current year's available
cash. Fortunately, in this company, the communications staff
not only reviewed preliminary financials, but actually helped
write the MD & A. When the potential problem was pointed out
to the controller's department, the statements were immediately altered so that the noncurrent portion of the write-off was
added back to current "cash flow from operations." Both approaches conformed with GAAP. Both had the same tax consequences. The revised version, however, communicated much
more clearly to the average investor.

Finally, we have a function that is almost never considered
part of the IR team, but can be one of its most constructive
members — pension fund and foundation management.

Most companies of any size have executives who oversee the
investment of hundreds of millions of pension and foundation
funds. Sometimes they are hands-on managers, making investment decisions themselves. In other cases, they select and
oversee outside managers who make the direct investment decisions. In either case, they are involved in the market day by day.
They must measure their performance against other fund managers. And they almost invariably *vote* the shares they hold
(much of it in their own company).

Clearly, most large companies have, in house, a group of
executives who are wired into Wall Street. At any given time,
they should know which funds may be interested in securities
similar to those issued by their employers, which probably have
no interest, and which are likely to be moving out of that kind of
security in the near future. They should be in an excellent
position to critique and help form their firm's IR marketing
program. They should be able to provide information on potential institutional investors. And, through their professional associations, they should be able to keep IR apprised of trends in
institutional voting on sensitive issues.

But, believe it or not, pension and foundation fund managers are seldom a routine, integral part of IR program planning
or program monitoring.

In summary:

• The Investor Relations title in most companies covers only a small part of the total function, usually the care and feeding of Wall Street's heavy hitters.
• Rating agency relations are seldom fully integrated into most IR programs, even though debt holders can be much more important to corporate survival in tough times than equity holders, and even though debt ratings can directly affect equity prices.
• Too often, financial statements and their notes are created without input from communications professionals, and are therefore unnecessarily difficult for investors to interpret. Often this is because communications professionals are not perceived as competent to help (see next section); that is generally the fault of the firm that employs them.
• Finally, pension fund and foundation management is seldom part of the corporate IR team despite the invaluable insights these experts can provide to any marketing-oriented IR effort. Normally, this is simply because they are never asked to participate.

The Image Merchants

In many companies, corporate communications is viewed as an area where style triumphs over substance. In nearly as many cases, this reputation may well be deserved. The fault, however, is generally not in the staff, but in the corporation's expectations of this subfunction.

Many companies view advertising, press relations, and associated disciplines as functions that "put a good face" on communications. Sometimes this means softening the impact of bad news or spreading glitter on even modest good news. Clearly, competent communications professionals have the technical capability to do this. But so do competent attorneys and accountants, each in their own way. And, at times, all these functions go overboard in such efforts. At best, what results is "hype." At worst, it can result in fraud.

However, most of the time companies avoid such excess. In fact, attorneys and accountants are expected to guard against hyperbole. For some reason, in many firms, communications professionals are not. They respond accordingly.

In addition, life other professionals, communications experts often have a tendency to become engrossed in their own techniques. In communications, this results in esoteric phrases such as "share of mind," or usually pointless dissertations on such things as "the creative use of white space." Interestingly, the amount of such "technobabble" one hears outside the communications department is often a clue as to how much style versus substance management expects from the function.

Let me illustrate this with a real-life example. I once sat in a high-level meeting where the president of a major corporate division presented a convoluted, ill-advised acquisition scheme to the heads of corporate staff departments. In his division, communications was strictly a "style" function. When he finished, he turned to the head of corporate communications and said, "Once this whore is ready to go, I want you to dress her up and take her to the dance." He fully expected an enthusiastic response, complete with comments on appropriate press interviews, brochures, speeches, and so on. At his division, that's exactly what would have happened.

At the corporate level, however, things were quite different. The head of corporate communications began to ask a series of pointed questions that exposed serious problems with the scheme. He knew his company's business. He knew his company's investors. He knew what they would accept, what they would question, and why. He was trained in the law, was well grounded in finance, and had 20 years' experience in communications. By the time he was finished, the project was quite properly dead in the water.

An extreme example perhaps, but one that clearly illustrates how management's expectations affect the depth of involvement of the communications function in any company. At the corporate level, management clearly expected, and received, much more substantive involvement from this function than was the case at the division in question. In fact, as result of this meeting, the CEO of the corporation took a personal interest in changing attitudes at that division.

Ideally, then, how does communications fit in? Whether one calls it communications or public relations, this group of functions in reality seeks to elicit from target audiences behavior that supports its employer's goals. In a marketing-oriented IR environment, this goal usually makes "hype" inadvisable. Since securities are in essence semidurable goods, the relationship sought is a long-term one, and unrealistic expectations are to be avoided. In fact, this is one area where attorneys, accountants, and communicators should have totally common purpose.

What communications brings to the party is twofold: first, an understanding of human motivation and behavior; second, a knowledge of communications techniques that can help elicit desired behavior.

The more involved the communications people are in market segmentation, the better they understand the target audiences, and the better able they are to develop effective communications channels to reach those audiences. The more involved they are in developing the primary information to be communicated (such as SEC documents and financial reports), the better they are able to properly distil that information into effective, credible messages in the form of advertisements, annual reports, press releases, or speeches.

In addition, because they make extensive use of both data and demographic research, communications professionals can contribute enormously to developing comparisons of a company with its peers, and in profiling both individual and institutional securities market segments.

However, at most firms, here is how it really works. Press relations is measured either by the amount of ink it generates or by the amount it doesn't generate. (Believe it or not, some companies hire press relations professionals to keep them out of the press.)

Corporate advertising either is an extension of product advertising or seeks to project some kind of "feel good" image about the company (or, in many cases, the CEO). Little thought is given to truly effective messages detailing the investment qualities of the firm.

Finally, annual and quarterly report production is mainly a matter of design, not substance. Far too often, the only "substantive" contribution communications makes is to pick a "theme" for the report — one year it features products, another year employees, and yet another year a nebulous theme such as "Poised for Tomorrow." Ironically, at many companies, substance is injected into shareholder reports only by placing them under the IR manager described in the preceding section. This can be effective, but can also result in publications written solely for securities analysts. It has the additional problem of even further reducing the direct involvement of communications people with investor issues.

All in all, as practiced at most firms, communications represents a real waste of a potentially powerful resource.

In summary:

• At many firms, communications is a "style" rather than "substance" function because that's what management expects.

• In fact, communications can be a powerful member of the IR team, identifying behavior and motivation patterns for target market segments; demystifying legal and accounting complexities; winnowing down data into messages designed to elicit supportive behavior; delivering those messages in the right form and through the right channels to generate maximum effectiveness; and closing the loop by monitoring a company's communications profile in comparison with that of peers in the investment community.

OK, SO HOW DO WE MAKE THIS THING WORK?

So far, we've looked at the shortcomings of ad hoc IR. We've defined IR as a marketing function. And, we've looked at the basic subfunctions that collectively make up true IR, in terms of both their shortfalls in normal practice and their potential contributions if properly structured. How can we use all of this to help us properly structure IR?

As I stated at the beginning of this chapter, there is no single, magic structure that works for all companies at all times. However, the key to good IR at any company is twofold: (1) a proper charter and (2) leadership.

The charter has been stated often in this chapter. We'll state it once more: *Investor relations is a marketing function that seeks to generate fair market value for a company's securities.*

In brief review, a marketing approach to IR makes the following assumptions:

1. The *product* is the potential for future economic gain an investor buys through the security in question (*not* the security or the company, per se).
2. The *customer base* is comprised of those segments of the institutional (portfolio manager) and individual investor population that seek economic gains from securities with the particular risk/reward/asset/line-of-business characteristics that come with ownership of the issuing firm's debt or equity securities.
3. The various reports (printed and otherwise) sent out to investors by companies are *marketing literature,* designed either to encourage a purchase or to maintain an ongoing customer relationship.
4. Securities analysts, the business and financial press, investment advisors, and brokers are *marketing conduits* that sometimes help move an investment story associated with a security to its target customers efficiently. They are very important, but they are actually creatures of the market, *not* the market itself.

Fair market value occurs when clear, concise information about a security's current status and its potential for future financial reward is distributed as thoroughly as possible among those segments of the investor population that represent that security's natural constituency at that time. These segments bidding against each other for the security generates fair value in the marketplace. Although this may seem a bit theoretical, it is simply a recasting of the immutable laws of supply and demand.

With this charge, and the proper leadership, all the members of the IR team can work together to segment the market, generate marketing information that is understandable while being legally and technically defensible, distribute that information through effective channels, and, most important, acquire ongoing feedback from the market on program effectiveness versus competing investments.

What, then, is the proper leadership structure? In purely theoretical terms, the form itself doesn't matter if it in fact assures that each piece of the IR puzzle understands its role in the marketing function and works cooperatively with other subfunctions under that umbrella concept.

As a practical matter, this ideal best achieved by having a single, marketing-oriented executive responsible for the function as described here. Where possible, reporting relationships should be direct (solid line). In some instances, however, a dotted-line relationship will have to do.

In every firm, the responsibility for IR clearly belongs to the CEO. However, in many cases the CEO may not be the best person to execute this charge, day to day. Regardless, although the authority for IR can be, and often is, delegated, the responsibility will always remain with the CEO.

If it is not practical for the CEO to fill the day-to-day executive duties, an excellent alternative is the executive responsible for strategic planning. This person knows the company intimately, is aware of its future plans and their economic potential, is probably marketing oriented, should have enough corporate clout to make dotted-line relationships work when they exist, and should be conversant with finance, law, and value analysis from an investor point of view. In fact, companies are more and more placing their entire IR/communications/shareholder relations operations under their strategic planning executive.

Is there no place for a more classic structure like the one charted earlier in this chapter? The answer is a provisional yes. But only if the CEO takes an extremely active role in focusing the IR function in the minds of the senior executives who oversee its parts. The CEO must demand a coordinated IR plan from the "team" and require regular reviews in which IR is the sole topic of discussion. The CEO is the team leader, and holds the group to their plan.

There is one final requirement, regardless of which managerial structure is chosen. I call it "top-down/bottom-up" delegation of duties. An initial delegation of duties must be developed, in writing, by the team itself, however it is organized. While the charter is set from the top, each subfunction is required to articulate its contribution to the program. The team members are encouraged at this stage to go beyond their traditional roles and propose additional contributions they could make to the program. This is where, for example, stockholder services could propose that they add demographic analysis to their responsibilities in order to aid in the market segmentation effort.

In concert with this effort a "resources" budget is developed that identifies not only staff and dollar needs, but information-access needs and requirements for interaction with other sub-functions in order to successfully perform the proposed funcions. These initial reports are collected at the top, collated, critiqued, and turned into a practical program. One more top-to-bottom-to-top pass ensues, allowing each subfunction to review its potential role in relation to those of the other members of the team and to comment on and critique this intermediate structure. The senior IR executive, or CEO-chaired senior committee, approves the final delegation of duties.

As a practical matter, this delegation of duties should be reviewed and revised *by the team* on a regular basis. The review can, in fact, be an integral part of annual budgeting. Properly executed, it can result in zero-based budgeting, rather than a routine "last-year-plus-inflation" budget process.

Perhaps the most important outfall of this kind of regular review of responsibility and authority of each subfunction within the overall IR function is a significant reduction in day-to-day turf battles. The battles are waged only once a year. Provided the CEO or the CEO's delegate is a strong, no-nonsense leader, the mutually agreed upon delegation of duties will tend to short-circuit most turf battles during the rest of the year. This can be especially important in times of crisis.

Throughout this chapter, we have discussed IR as the primary purview of the CEO. At this time, that is clearly the case. In closing, let me suggest that the future may hold a somewhat different structure for IR.

In fact, the CEO works for the board of directors. The board, in turn, is elected by shareholders. For many companies, this relationship has long been something of a fiction. In fact, the

CEO runs the show, with the board providing some supervision but mostly supporting the CEO's initiatives. Shareholders exert their authority only rarely.

As we know, this is rapidly changing. Investors are becoming more active and forcing boards to become more active in turn. At the moment, few boards are directly involved in IR. However, some associations specializing in corporate governance are seriously investigating the creation of special board committees that would provide shareholders a direct communications channel to a company's independent directors.

A rational alternative would be to establish a board/IR relationship similar to the current board/auditor relationship. Clearly, some CEOs would consider this a severe erosion of their authority. I believe, however, such a relationship may well become widespread over the next decade.

Let me close with two thoughts. First, all a CEO's authority is, in fact, delegated to him or her by the board. Second, those CEOs who would object to IR/board interaction should consider whether or not they might find it an intriguing idea at firms where they are outside directors. After all, IR's primary responsibility is generating fair market value for a company's securities. Is that not a prime charge to each and every board of a publicly held company, as well?

* * * * *

Johnnie D. Johnson is executive vice president and a managing director of Georgeson & Company, a financial relations and proxy solicitation firm. He served as director of investor relations for several major corporations and was chairman of the National Investor Relations Institute.

SENIOR MANAGEMENT'S ROLE IN AN EFFECTIVE INVESTOR RELATIONS PROGRAM

Alyn V. Essman
CPI Corporation

To be effective, investor relations (IR) must be a function of personal communications. Although the goal of an IR program is to build awareness and understanding of the company, experience dictates, in this as in any other undertaking, that communication and understanding are human functions that can be accomplished only between people. As the chief interpreter of corporate policy, a capable CEO places his personal imprint on the IR program, and the impressions that emanate from that communication should and will bear the personal stamp of the human interpreter. In that sense, it's critically important that the CEO and the CEO's chosen corporate spokesperson adopt an attitude of personal identification with the program rather than neutral objectivity.

My observations, then, are based on personal experience in the development and implementation of CPI's IR program, and, as such, rest on empirical analysis and practical experience rather than on a study of many other corporate programs. That experience, though, includes observations of other corporate spokespeople and exposure to many different kinds of internal and external corporate communications.

Overseeing IR fits easily within my view of the CEO's functions. Generally, the functional responsibilities of a CEO include providing guidance and direction for the corporation and facilitating its development along those lines through the motivation of its officers. This calls for the CEO to plan and prepare the road to progress, remove obstacles, and report and interpret the results to the corporation's many constituencies. The constituencies of the corporation include its customers and employees as well as its suppliers and investors. Considering the CEO's functional responsibilities in this light, it's easy to see how the IR program dovetails with the CEO's daily responsibilities.

When one recognizes the investing public as an important constituency of the company, one naturally views the function of cultivating good IR as a legitimate part of the CEO's job description and supports it enthusiastically. For those CEOs, however, who consider IR to be a distracting chore, frustration and irritation replace enthusiasm and detract from the effectiveness of communication. To be effective, dialogue with concerned investors must be open, candid, and forthcoming — not forced.

The prime function of the CEO — guidance and direction — implies goal setting, and effective goal setting requires active dialogue. An initial statement of objectives should be modified in response to reaction and feedback from employees and/or stockholders. By responding and reacting to intelligent feedback, an effective CEO will be better able to communicate objectives and confirm his and the company's dedication to goals and principles. This give and take through open dialogue establishes a clear image of mutually acceptable goals and objectives Better understanding fosters continuity of purpose and provides for consistency of presentation. Through open dialogue, the corporate spokesperson can establish a cultural foundation supporting integrity and dedication to the accepted principles.

This kind of dialogue is also effective within the company in establishing internal incentive plans based on these same goals and objectives, which can also form a statement of corporate purpose. The IR program is a natural extension of the same types of communication with current or prospective investors. The CEO who endorses open dialogue internally will find a very comfortable extension through external channels.

Effective external communication requires an open line to customers and suppliers for the transmission of ideas and attitudes that should be in consonance with internal communication among management and employees about the company's goals and the potential rewards for achieving those goals. Stockholders, investors, and lenders also must understand the corporate philosophy in order to support the corporate culture. By integrating these various communication channels into a coordinated network, one can create an image of consistency and continuity that reflects the corporate personality. Although the extension of this concept to legal and regulatory agencies requires some adaptation, I believe that the same elements of candor and honesty should govern those communications as well. The difficulties that one frequently experiences with the regulatory bureaucracy can often be overcome by a wholesome attitude of openness and candor.

One of the major objectives of any company is to improve its position in the marketplace — to earn a profit and to have profits accurately reflected in the company's stock price. An IR program developed along these guidelines should foster that objective. Profit is recognized in its most general terms as an improvement in the company's "balance sheet," which represents the economic value created and enjoyed by the company. In a real sense, then, the market evaluation of a company is a form of value — a proprietary currency. Not only is it important to create the accounting value recognized on the books and records, but it is equally as important to translate that into a realistic market valuation. Consequently, a fair and equitable, but not falsely inflated, stock price should be one of the objectives of enlightened corporate management.

One must recognize that value is not merely a function of static economic measurement but also relates to the liquidity of an investment. In that sense, a fluid trading market is essential to maintaining a realistic stock price. A meaningful and informative IR program is one of the ways in which corporate performance can be interpreted by the investing public so as to facilitate market liquidity and price responsiveness.

Completing the cycle, proprietary currency in the form of market valuation serves as a vehicle for continuing growth. A fair stock price and a fluid market provide easy access to capital markets and enhance the value of stock as currency to facilitate acquisition programs. Finally, and certainly not unimportant in our achievement-oriented society, fair stock pricing and fluid trading serve as motivating score cards for management and employees. The psychological value of market recognition through these measurements cannot be overstated. In fact, it's that very psychological drive which sometimes creates a distorted IR program that goes beyond the appropriate requirements of open communication.

An effective IR program requires commitment. Implementation of an IR program is no different from any other responsibility assumed by the CEO and his staff. It deserves a full measure of attention as part of the CEO's functional responsibility. It requires structural integration and coordination with other CEO activities in such a fashion that it can be woven into the fabric of executive attitudes and decision making. An IR program that's appended or hung on as an afterthought will earn the little respect and attention that its position deserves.

This does not mean that IR is and must be the personal preserve of the CEO. Investor relations activities can and should be delegated as appropriate. Consulting advisors can help manage the channels of communication and provide access to specific tools of the trade. The CEO's responsibility is to initiate the process, interpret feedback, and evaluate the performance of the implementing officer or consultant. Only under the direction of the CEO, however, can the company properly implement a sound IR policy. In the early formative years, hands-on, direct guidance from the CEO is imperative. This is the development phase, where the tone of the program should be established to reflect the corporate personality and provide the coordination with other communications programs. Once the format is established, though, the IR staff can continue and expand the program. In that same sense, advisors can offer aid and counsel, but the use of advisors as operators or implementors is an abdication that dooms the program to mockery or failure.

Making an IR program effective requires developmental effort and interpretative skill. Investor relations goes far beyond the presentation of raw data. Investor attitudes should be based on operating statistics but can be meaningful only if those statistics are interpreted and integrated with a coherent statement of corporate philosophy using appropriate assessments of progress. The CEO or IR executive should be willing to accept the risk of interpretation without forcing conclusions. Prohibitions against the dissemination of inside information and the existence of regulatory disclosure requirements should dictate caution but not silence. Failure to disclose can be much more misleading than a thoughtful explanation of current events in the context of long-term plans.

We've never felt, at CPI, that it's necessary to offer specific forecasts or to carefully monitor analysts' earnings projections. We consider it our responsibility, however, to provide sufficient information and interpretation of the available data to allow analysts to build credible earnings models and, using their own evaluative techniques, to predict logical scenarios.

When conflicts of analysis arise, it's incumbent upon company spokespeople to provide sufficient interpretation and background to assist in resolving those conflicts and to display a continuity of corporate purpose and objectives through the development of credible information.

Interpretation, though, should stop short of selling. It's not the function of an IR program to sell stock, but rather to provide a liquid market for investors through general dissemination of information about the company. An objective outlook is particularly important. Investment and/or divestiture of stock should not be considered a vote for or against the company but should be recognized as a prudent investor's reaction to market fluctuations. A liquid market is far more important than the permanent placement of stock in the hands of long-term investors. The poorly informed investor with a long-term outlook quickly becomes a seller in the event of an unexplained or unexpected change of corporate fortunes. An educated investor has the ability to differentiate between a transition and a reversal and that knowledge can form a basis for confidence in the company's ability to manage the transition successfully.

In pursuit of liquidity, a broad constituency is highly valuable. One not only should communicate with stockholders or friendly analysts, but should be available to speak to local communities and national and local media as well as to educational institutions and investment bankers. Making the company spokesperson available to the press and maintaining a visible profile in the local and national community provide a base of support for a company's IR efforts. Regular communication with analysts broadens the base of support and softens the edge of the interface with the financial community. An analyst who speaks with knowledge about a company speaks with authority. A regular schedule of planned meetings with analysts further serves these purposes.

Coordination, then, is the key to effective communications. An IR program should offer group meetings and face-to-face encounters with individual investors and prospects. Press releases should go beyond the presentation of summarized operating results to provide valuable background material. Communications should be frequent and dependable. It's good to establish a format that breeds understanding and familiarity with the company's attitudes and philosophy. Press releases are at least as important in the recitation of adverse circumstances as in the trumpeting of accomplishments and achievements. No company and/or individual is without fault or flaw. An informed investor who understands the reason and character of a growth interruption is better able to cope with problems as they occur.

In order to present a clear picture, the corporation should speak with a unified voice to all constituencies. Corporate annual reports and quarterly reports need to adopt a different point of view from corporate internal communications, but the general message should be consistent in image and philosophy. Sometimes it helps to translate the same message for delivery to different channels. For instance, the information presented in regulatory documents can be rephrased and reinterpreted to foster a healthy employee communications program reinforcing the image the company adopts in a sound IR program. Financial presentations should be generalized to serve more than one purpose. Repetition of similar information in slightly different formats creates a harmonic resonance that enhances the credibility of the company's story. The fact that a company projects a consistent image through different channels reinforces the feeling of integrity. These coordinating functions can be successful only under the firm guidance of a capable, full-charge CEO.

Investor relations, in summary, is a significant part of a company's goal setting, strategic planning, and growth programming. As such, it demands attention and involvement of the CEO and his staff to assure consonance with and relevance to corporate goals. When viewed in the context of the CEO's overall responsibility to guide and direct the company over the paths of progress, the IR program becomes a natural part of day-to-day responsibilities. By allowing his or her personality to influence the communications and by buying into the active dialogue, the CEO makes the IR program not only a healthy contributor to proprietary corporate currency and value, but also a worthwhile and enjoyable dialogue.

* * * * *

Alyn V. Essman is chairman and CEO of CPI Corp., in St. Louis. The investor relations industry recognizes him for his balanced and committed view of corporate officers' responsibilities to shareholders.

INVESTOR RELATIONS: THE USER'S PERSPECTIVE

Peter C. Lincoln
United States Steel and Carnegie Pension Fund

This chapter first outlines the purpose that an investor relations (IR) program can fulfill as part of overall management objectives and then gives several elements of an effective program, including the need for a concise and realistic discussion of past results and future goals and challenges. The present lack of informative business segment statistics and commentary at many companies is highlighted. Suggestions are given for structuring a coordinated program of written reports, company presentations, and management visits, with negative comments offered on summary reporting. Suggestions are made to help reduce insider information risks. Finally, comments are provided on how the IR function can be executed and improved.

WHAT PURPOSE IR?

There are some obvious reasons why companies must support an IR effort. A public company must comply with an array of legal, securities markets, and fiduciary requirements to report the results of enterprise performance quarterly and annually, and to disseminate additional information in a timely manner if there has been any material change in prospects of the organization since previously published reports. The IR function provides continuity to the organization and dissemination of corporate reporting information, and acts as the focal point for questions from stockholders about the organization.

Beyond the legal and administrative requirements, however, the IR program can and should provide a positive contribution to the organization through enhancing the likelihood that the company's debt and equity securities will be properly and realistically valued over time and by reducing the potential volatility of the securities during periods of company or general market instability. Many security analysts believe that stock and bond prices of an individual company can achieve more appropriate levels in the marketplace when the organization's operations and management strategies are properly understood, and as credibility is gained through a consistent communications process. These conditions should also reduce the impact of "surprises" and unexpected events, since investors will be able to understand such events in the context of the company's strengths and management's capacity to address potential problems. If these conditions of understanding and credibility can be achieved, along with appropriate market recognition, the cost of capital to the organization can be reduced, and enterprise performance has been improved. If securities prices reach appropriate levels of recognition in the markets, stockholder objectives are better achieved, and the possibility of hostile outside takeovers is reduced.

Some important indirect benefits with employees and customers can also come from an effective IR program. Many employees participate in stock option or company savings programs, and these programs better achieve their objectives if the prices of the company's securities reach realistic performance levels and are not volatile. Stockholder reports that succeed in communicating company results and management goals can also be among the most effective channels for communicating such goals to employees, leading to a better internal sense of direction and focus. An effective communications program can also enhance customer relationships. Potential customers routinely look at a company's financial reports when making business decisions, and a clear and credible discussion of operations can have a positive impact on such matters.

ELEMENTS OF AN EFFECTIVE IR PROGRAM

The establishment of management and enterprise credibility, a prime objective of an effective IR program, must start with a realistic and forthright discussion of a company's past and current performance. At least six years of financial data in appropriate detail must be provided in the annual report in order to give perspective over varying economic and business cycles, and the management discussion should give a realistic explanation for whatever performance was achieved during the period. Unusual gains or losses should be noted, and ongoing performance excluding these items should be the basis for discussion, as analysts are strongly interested in underlying revenue and earnings trends rather than just reported results.

A realistic discussion of the company's present competitive position, the strategies for the future in current operations, and the possibility for adding new businesses or eliminating current ones should be outlined. The means of achieving these goals, including how they will be financed, as well as the risks and uncertainties involved, are critical for investor understanding of these objectives. The financial goals of the company, including capital structure, return on equity, and dividend payout policy, should be outlined in annuals and in company presentations.

The erratic quality of business segment reporting has been of serious concern to security analysts for many years. A company operating in more than one business segment cannot expect to gain investor confidence unless the operations in each segment are discussed clearly and sufficient financial data are provided to compare these segments with other companies operating in those industries. Although annual segment data have been required for some years, the Securities and Exchange Commission, at this writing, has deferred a ruling that this information be provided quarterly. Security analysts, through the Financial Analysts Federation, have strongly criticized this deferral. Any company that obscures its results by not providing segment data is creating an immediate credibility problem with investors, raising a clear possibility that the securities may not achieve full recognition of the underlying values in the securities markets. Many companies that do provide annual and quarterly segment data run these same risks when the segment material is not produced on a valid line-of-business basis but rather is given in broader aggregates not truly reflecting realistic industry categories. A major flaw in some segment reporting is the misuse of the category "Other," either as a miscellaneous segment itself or through the use of an "Other Expense" item that masks the pretax earnings items by segment through an artificial allocation of general overhead or other elements.

Clarity and conciseness should be important objectives for an effective IR program. Many companies provide a wealth of data, but do so in an unorganized and diffuse manner, so that it is only the rare analyst, able to devote hours to reading one company's material, who can gain full benefit from the exercise. The starting point to improve the effectiveness of the communications process is the chairman's letter in the annual quarterly reports. The key analytical points relating to past performance, be it good or bad, and the important strategies and problems for the future should be summarized in that portion of the reports and then discussed in greater detail in the management discussion section. The absence of a strong focal point in the annual and quarterly reports is consistently the weakest area in all IR programs.

The importance of having a concise and clear outline of company performance and strategies, perhaps always obvious, is today becoming increasingly obligatory as a consequence of the limited amount of time that an investment analyst or individual investor has to focus on any one company. There has been a bewildering explosion of publicly traded issues and new financial instruments such as futures and options. Evolving investment strategies, such as sector rotation and asset allocation, have lessened the time and effort that an individual analyst can spend on any one company. At the same time, some large institutional departments seem to have been shifted from maintaining a staff of seasoned fundamental security analysts to greater investment decision making on the part of a growing population of portfolio managers. An increasing amount of institutional money is being managed by investment advisory firms that do not maintain traditional research departments. All this suggests that the traditional security analyst has even less time to do serious research, and, as portfolio managers themselves rely on their own investigation, they too will have only a limited amount of time to review any one company. Consequently, the basic company message must be communicated clearly and concisely, in a substantive and professional manner; if it is not, the message will never reach its destination.

Finally, the strong endorsement and participation of the CEO, as well as of other members of senior management, are critical to the success of an IR program. The CEO is ultimately responsible for corporate performance and, along with the board of directors, must formulate and execute the company's business strategies and determine the financial goals. The understanding of these elements is essential to a security analyst's opinion on the investment, and this can only be achieved if the strategies are prominently included in the published materials and communicated personally by the chief executive at company presentations and in interviews. It must also be said, as a practical matter, that lower-level officers are often reluctant to talk frankly or realistically about past performance if the chief executive has not already done so in stockholder reports or company presentations. As suggested earlier, if the company is to achieve credibility and appropriate recognition for its securities, there must have occurred over time a candid discussion of past performance as well as future risks, and if the CEO has not made sure that this has been done, the effectiveness of the IR program is in some doubt.

STRUCTURE OF AN IR PROGRAM

The structure of an effective IR program will vary according to the size and nature of the enterprise, but it should involve a coordinated and consistently executed program of required written reports, public presentations, and personal visits between security analysts and senior management.

Written Reports

The annual and quarterly reports to stockholders represent the most important communication channel with analysts as well as with individual investors, employees, potential customers, and other interested parties. While these reports must cover various matters as required by the SEC and other regulatory agencies, management has considerable latitude to shape them into an effective vehicle for communicating substantive financial and business strategy issues, as well as general information about the company's operations.

Many of the important ingredients for good annual and quarterly reports have been outlined. Management should be realistic and forthright when discussing past performance, as well as goals and strategies for the future. The statistical data and the management discussion in the annual report should embrace at least six years of operations in order to provide perspective over an economic or business cycle period. Business segment data should give a fair representation of the real operations of the organization, and the data should not be muddied by arbitrary and misleading use of categories such as "Other Expenses" or "Other General Allocations." Unusual or nonrecurring gains and losses should be identified on both a pretax and aftertax basis, so that the reader can get some feeling for underlying operating trends. When purchase accounting acquisitions have occurred, the various revenue and expense items should be discussed on a before-and-after-acquisition basis, again so that ongoing trends can be understood; a similar process should occur with regard to balance sheet factors. When pooling mergers have occurred, per-share data should be given as originally reported as well as on the restated basis.

Management should respond quickly to investor concerns — providing data to enable outsiders to assess unusual events rather than attempting to avoid new disclosures. Although some requests for new data can be bothersome, the importance of addressing investor concerns on a timely basis, thereby limiting the volatility and uncertainty in the securities markets, should be a far more important criterion for senior management than the time it might take for a few employees to develop certain data.

The annual report should be the most complete document published by a company, and is often enhanced through publication of an annual statistical supplement. Although the quarterly reports cover less data, it is still important for the company to provide a good amount of financial detail on a quarterly basis in the same format as used in the annuals, including good business segment data. The management discussion should also provide commentary on business segment concerns, and the chairman's report should give a substantive summary of financial results in the quarter as well as discuss any important business events affecting the enterprise. A summary of comments made at the annual meeting as well as the outcome of any votes should either be sent to stockholders and investors as a separate publication or be included in the first quarter report. The IR function should also make available on a routine basis to those who desire it copies of the proxy form, the 10-K and 10-Q reports, and any 8-Ks and other filings of substance.

As of this writing, the Financial Executives Institute is continuing to lobby for what is called *summary reporting*. Although the methodology and motivation of this concept have never been clear, the concept involves the ability of management to select elements of the annual report, including even the financial statements, to be abridged into a summary report that would be sent to all stockholders. If stockholders so desired, they could then send for the full 10-K report to get the complete story. This raises some serious legal issues with regard to selective disclosure in company reports and to circumstances where certain investors on special lists would receive what might be material information several days or even weeks ahead of other stockholders. Questions also arise as to the appropriateness of the company management determining which aspects of SEC disclosure requirements or certified financial statements should be made available on a timely basis to stockholders. Summary reporting also introduces a cumbersome proliferation of published reports and further complicates the information-gathering burdens of investment analysts making initial assessments of companies whose reports are not currently being obtained. Summary reporting potentially also raises credibility issues that may well harm rather than enhance the company's ability to be appropriately valued in the market.

Public Presentations

It is important for senior managements to make public presentations to investor groups on a periodic and reasonably consistent basis. No matter how well written reports may discuss a company's performance and plans for the future, many analysts will absorb the information more readily on hearing it. By attending a meeting, analysts make a much greater commitment of time and concentration than by merely reading the financials. Investors are interested in judging the character and depth of management, particularly on how well they handle questions and answers; and the opportunity to ask questions can induce a much greater understanding of a company than otherwise. Many investors do not have the time or ability to travel to company offices, so that these meetings provide the best way to become well-acquainted with a particular operation.

There are several approaches that can be taken to public presentations, depending on the nature and size of the company. The most obvious approach is to address one of the 54 member societies of the Financial Analysts Federation located throughout the nation. The most important, because of the concentration of institutional investors, are New York, Boston, and Chicago, and for specific companies other societies near headquarters or important plant locations should also be considered. There are also a large number of specialty industry "splinter" groups, to whose meetings companies in specific industries are often invited, and whose members usually also belong to the Financial Analysts Federation. Other presentations can be made at company annual meetings, at meetings sponsored by investment banking firms or brokers, or at meetings organized by the company.

The content of the company presentations normally reflect the comments made earlier about the annual report. A discussion of past performance and the factors producing poor or good results, as well as strategies for the future and an outline of important financial goals are normally the focus of such a presentation. The CEO and CFO would naturally be part of this program, and other division heads or important staff specialists could be included depending on circumstances and investor interests. The question and answer part of the meeting is considered significant by analysts as an opportunity to assess management personalities and responsiveness to concerns.

Personal Visits with Investors and Analysts

The nature of a personal visitation program will vary with the institution, but for many it can involve a mixture of addressing the needs of analysts and investors for "maintenance" information, and a more active program of seeking out potential investors. Some brokerage house specialists and institutional investors with internal analytical staffs need to maintain a level of knowledge about many companies, and will speak with management by phone, by visiting with management in their own offices, or at company headquarters. With an increasing number of investment and research decisions made by portfolio managers rather than traditional security analysts, the importance of a coordinated program of senior management and/or the IR executive calling on potential institutional investors is growing. Once this effort has started, follow-up calls and visits should be considered as a means of retaining the attention of the prospective investor.

AVOIDING THE INSIDER TRADING TRAP

The number of insider trading scandals has grown in recent years, with many of them emanating from mergers and acquisitions, arbitrage, and other corporate finance functions. However, it has long been recognized that there is a potential conflict of interest for security analysts and the IR function between a legitimate desire on the part of the analyst for a good understanding of the operations of the company on the one hand, and the risks of obtaining important information about the company that has not generally been disclosed to others.

The best way for the company to reduce its potential insider trading problem is to do a thorough and forthright job in the published stockholder reports — identifying problems and opportunities, future risks and uncertainties, and important strategies and policies, so that outsiders can make their own assessments given their outlook for the economy and a specific business.

One important area where companies risk serious conflicts is business segment reporting. Those companies that do not publish segment breakdowns on a quarterly basis, or do so in a manner that obscures real results, are especially vulnerable if they discuss specific divisional results with analysts in personal conversations. Some companies excuse this practice by saying that they would talk on this basis with anybody who calls, but of course the problem is that many do not know that such an opportunity actually exists. Although segment reporting does require more work, it also conforms with the spirit of public-disclosure practices, and does so on a basis that is fair for all investors, be they large or small.

Company management and the IR person must also guard against providing sensitive information to specific individuals, whom they have come to know and trust over the years, to the exclusion of other investors. There is naturally a question of judgment as to what constitutes information that is beyond what might legitimately be given to a thorough analyst, but this is a question that should be consciously weighed by management as it carries out these functions.

THE IR POSITION

The IR position can be one of the most interesting staff functions in a corporation. In a small company, this function may be handled by the CEO or the CFO, but if this role is delegated to an IR person, the function is one of the few in the organization below the top management level whose scope embraces the entire organization rather than specific line departments. The nature of the responsibility means that the individual chosen must have some knowledge of accounting, finance, and industry conditions, but must also possess general intelligence and a conceptual sense of how the organization operates in order to be able to communicate effectively with security analysts and portfolio managers.

The mandate for the IR person should be to organize a broad and integrated corporate communications program for the company — not simply to play a passive role by reacting only to questions from outside. Such a position would involve a direct role in shaping the content of the written reports, organizing a program of public presentations, and meeting with investors, either alone or with key executives. While other departments would also be involved in these tasks, these participants must be aware of the existence of an organized, intelligent program and the reasons why such a program is important to the success of the company. A further mandate for the IR person is to be sensitive to investor concerns about the company, and to ensure that senior management promptly is made aware of such concerns and is responsive to the issues raised.

As suggested before, the participation by the CEO and senior department heads in the IR effort is quite important. Although many questions can be addressed directly by an informed IR person, there are also certain subjects that can only be discussed by specific managers or the chief executive, and the IR person should never respond to questions that are beyond his or her area of knowledge or expertise. Just as a company must establish credibility, so must the IR contact, and analysts can quickly become disenchanted if they are given poor answers or are prevented from speaking directly with knowledgeable executives.

Promptness is essential in responding to questions. Analysts have little time to focus on one company in small chapters or over several days, and unexpected news or false rumors need to be addressed quickly, before damage is done because of poor information in the market.

The availability of detailed information on a timely basis is also critical when quarterly and year-end earnings are announced. Analysts and investors need to know quickly why reported earnings went either up or down, and, in a company of any size, the reason can often be complicated. If the analyst has to wait a few weeks before certain data are produced by the company, interest can wane or important opportunities can be lost to make informed investment decisions in a rapidly changing market. The lack of detailed financial information at the time earnings are reported can also lead to insider-trading abuses; for instance, analysts may gain knowledge about certain aspects of earnings from informal conversations with various company officials before such information is available to the general public.

Finally, there are several outside sources of assistance for IR persons in assessing the quality of their program, such as public relations firms, some of which are specializing increasingly in investor relations, and the National Investor Relations Institute, a growing trade group in this area that sponsors seminars and other meetings. The Corporate Information Committee of the Financial Analysts Federation evaluates the IR program of companies in many specific industries, and publishes an annual report on its findings. Members of this committee are available for visits with individual companies to make further comments.

CONCLUSION

Investor relations is a critical area of senior management responsibility that never can be taken for granted. Results and prospective challenges must be discussed promptly, concisely, and realistically during good times and bad, both in written reports to shareholders and through a consistent program of company presentations and visits with analysts and investors. These efforts will enable security analysts and others to understand more readily a company's businesses, and this better understanding should lead to more realistic and less volatile pricing of the securities of the organization.

* * * * *

Peter C. Lincoln is vice president of investments for United States Steel and Carnegie Pension Fund. He is also former chairman of the Corporate Information Committee of the Financial Analysts Federation.

DETERMINING AND
DELIVERING THE IR MESSAGE

Earl Merkel
Earl Merkel Communications Group

My mother-in-law — a recently retired teacher — quotes Louis Rukeyser to me. My travel agent, whose corporate secretarial sources provide her with information most arbitrageurs would kill for, cites PE ratios and comments knowledgeably on restructuring activities at selected companies. And recently, while sharing a cab with several other business travelers, I witnessed a three-way dispute over the relative merits of a particular ISO — an argument involving an investment banker, a reporter for a national business magazine, and the driver of the cab.

Things have, to underscore the obvious, changed, and it is no exaggeration to say that the increased emphasis on the corporate Investor Relations (IR) function has been both cause and effect of much of this change.

Investor relations has moved from a purely informational, numbers-heavy, and task-oriented job to a comprehensive financial and marketing communications profession — one which requires technical competence and management expertise. In a growing number of successful companies, the IR function has become a policy-making function and an important part of the strategic planning process.

Simply defined, IR exists to send the proper messages to the proper audiences to obtain a desired action that supports progress toward a defined corporate strategic objective. Understanding this basic role is vital; achieving success depends on applying that role definition to the three essential factors in investor communications: the audience, the message, and the media.

The audience has changed: While institutional shareholders continue to dominate the attention (and, some say, dictate the actions) of the corporate entity, the investment game is now being played in prime time before an audience numbering in the millions. The much-heralded "return of the individual investor" may or may not be in large part hyperbole, but there is no debate that — prior to the October 1987 shocks — individual holdings had been growing at a rate not seen since the mid-20s and 60s. The enduring popularity of the ESOP and the emerging interest in recapitalizations that result in substantial employee equity are creating a new class of "owner-employees" who are interested in, and demanding of, detailed financial disclosure from management. In addition, all this has increased media scrutiny of (and market reaction to) corporate actions and events that previously would have brought minimal attention. Today, more and more individuals and groups are demanding not just more information, but materials explaining even the most basic financial information in simple and clear language.

The message also has changed: Not too long ago, there would have been very little discussion about the role of the IR function in determining the "messages" an IR program should (or would) send. The driving force was the SEC and its regulations, and the modus operandi of many organizations was to limit investor communications to what was mandated. This was, mind, before Mssrs. Boesky and Wynams helped move corporate finance from the business section and onto both the news columns and, courtesy of *Doonesbury,* the comics page.

And the medium has changed: The slick-looking, elegant annual report remains the flagship of the IR function, but it is by no means the sole choice available. Aware that different audiences respond differently to different vehicles, cognizant that the vehicle itself can send distinct messages, and understanding that every available vehicle has its own set of communications strengths and weaknesses, the IR functionary can today command an impressive arsenal.

As a result of today's emphasis on market-oriented communications, effective IR programs require ongoing evaluation of strategies and tactics, messages and media, audiences and delivery methodology. The result has been increased IR attention to sophisticated message determination and strategy-based decisions on communications vehicles — all based on the understanding that financial information is a resource to be employed for specific benefits.

And as with all resources, information has value only in how well it is employed to reach a further goal. A media release on quarterly earnings, a 10-K, even the image-rich annual report — in every aspect of our communications, we employ our information resource with a desired end in mind. Just how effective a communications project (or program) will be is, in large part, determined by how valuable this "end" is to the organization.

The goal of an annual report, for instance, can be as limited as "keeping the SEC off our backs." A media release may be written so as to make the dissemination of earnings information secondary to the practice of organizational politics — for instance, to stroke the ego of the chief financial officer by putting his or her name in the newspaper. Such minimal goals are the hallmark of poor communications programs and inept communications managers.

The recent spate of merger and acquisition activities has illustrated the value of IR's new corporate status. There are three attributes common to every company that has, in the past five years, successfully fought off the unwanted suitor:

1. It operated in an efficient and effective way.
2. Its activities created something of value, in one or another manner.
3. It successfully communicated points 1 and 2 to the critical investment audiences.

Point three will not go unnoticed by the discerning CEO, but the intelligent IR professional should not postpone pointing it out to the less acute corporate leader. Having an effective IR program is no guarantee against a determined, intelligent adversary, but not having one makes a successful defense as likely as drawing a perfect circle with an Etch-A-Sketch.

The essence of successful IR is the quest for mutual satisfaction: We strive to help the investor feel that he, she, or (with the committee-managed institutional portfolios around today) "it" has all the relevant information upon which to base a buy/ sell/hold decision. At the same time, our efforts are aimed at ensuring that the issuer of the securities in question — our company — knows that those buy/sell/hold decisions are being made on the basis of equitable responses to reasonable, logical, and predictable criteria.

Presumably, aside from the rather desirable objective of complying with reporting requirements and hence avoiding incarceration, the idea behind spending money on IR is to help persuade one or another of our organization's financial audiences to do something the organization wants done or to think in a way the organization needs it to think.

That's the strategic focus, and everything else — the elegant look of our annual report, the rousing background theme music to those corporate TV spots, the quality of the surf 'n turf served at the analysts meeting — are merely the tactics we select to send the messages that support organization strategy.

This is a tough job, at best. It's an impossible one if we forget the three essential ingredients of successful IR communications: the audience, the message, and the media.

AUDIENCE

Different people have staggeringly different interests and concerns; upon this precept is built almost every part of effective corporate communications. In IR, we must have a firm sense of whom we are addressing. A shareholder group with a high percentage of employees has a definite and predictable predisposition: It wants to hear how certain management actions will influence job security and employment stability, even at the expense of details regarding profitability. The garden-variety institutional shareholder — notoriously more fickle than the individual holding your company's shares — tends to focus on short-term operating actions and results. At the same time, the individual shareholder is usually heavily influenced by his or her broker, an individual who (when pressed) occasionally admits to being driven almost as much by the need to stimulate account activity as by the desire to maximize client return. In varying degrees of influence, the stockbroker (and more important, the brokerage house that employs numbers of this species) can have a leveraged effect on the buying and selling activity of a sizable group of individual shareholders.

There are audience motivations that transcend the profit motive, and the IR professional ignores them at his or her own peril. The socially conscious shareholder — either individual or institutional — is focused on certain social or ideological concerns: for example, South Africa is not a new issue; and both GE and Dow found, at the height of anti-Vietnam activism, an increasingly vocal shareholder attending annual meetings.

In all this, there is no substitute for good research. Who holds your shares? How are they likely to react in whatever scenarios are possible in your industry or situation? Is there a geographical or regional bias to consider? All in all, who *are* these people, and what *motivates* them?

Knowing your audience, as all this is tritely called, is a rule honored more in the breech than in the observance. Most IR types assume they do know their shareholders; what they actually mean is that they know the identity of their five largest shareholders. This failing is one reason crisis communications is such an active field these days. Size of holding is certainly a factor in planning good IR; whether it is *the* decisive factor or even on your list of the top ten concerns facing the IR program is the big question. You simply don't know unless you expend the effort required to find out.

Most corporations order regular computer analyses from their transfer agents or internal tracking functionary, reviewing cause-and-effect of stock sales, purchases, and other relevant market movement. But all too few invest in regular, timely, attitudinal and demographic studies, including focus groups and surveys of their shareholders and the professional counselors who influence shareholding entities. Such research, while more expensive than dream interpretation or mere guesswork about the likes and dislikes of your firm's legal owners, tends to provide a more credible basis for both anticipating and responding to what otherwise might become a critical IR situation.

The reason for all this intelligence gathering is not just so IR can give any particular shareholder audience exactly what it might think it wants to have. That's part of it, of course — after all, these are the corporation's *owners* we're discussing here. But even the most innocent IR practitioner might see the occasional need to use this kind of information to send a message that elicits a response desired by the corporation's *management*. And that brings us to the second essential, the message.

MESSAGE

I have a friend who is treasurer and CFO of a medium-size manufacturer of metal tubing. Over the past decade, he estimates that he's perused perhaps a thousand annual reports, his own company's and those of others. And over drinks, he confesses that he seldom reads the first half of an annual report — the so-called front of the book, which contains all the charts, photographs, management letters, and text that occupy so much of the time and attention of the IR professional.

He doesn't see the value of it.

"All that stuff is just window dressing," he told me. "Everything you need to know — everything that is *important* about the performance and operations of a company — is in the back of the report, right there in the numbers."

Arguably, he's right. Certainly, the reporting regulations enforced by the government seem to bear out this philosophy; there are reams of rules detailing the way we must report our numbers, but I have yet to find an SEC regulation requiring full-color portraits of the CEO on page 3.

But my friend misses the point. Like so many other financial technicians, he is confusing information distribution with message-sending. "Just the facts, ma'am" works fine for Jack Webb, but successful IR requires a more sophisticated approach to the communications process.

We're in the business of sending messages, first and foremost. Like all good managers, our job is to determine what *end result* our organization desires. Given that, we determine what we need to say to any specific audience that will result in that audience doing, thinking, or remembering something that supports the organization's progress toward the aforementioned end result. However, it makes little sense to send a message that nobody cares about. It's a sad fact, but human nature is such that people will respond only to information that addresses their own interests and concerns. In short, message and audience are inexorably linked. We must consider what it is we want to say, and target the group we expect will care about — or act upon — it.

What is it you want an audience to do, or think, or remember? Without fail, the answer is in the objectives of your organization's strategic plan.

Are these operating objectives? If so, your messages will focus on engineering, production, or service abilities. Are they financial in nature? Your focus probably moves to the management skills your company demands and develops. Are the objectives instead, as seems to be the trend today, more esoteric and "cultural"? Your messages will then likely focus on "people" qualities and how these "fit" in terms of your operating and financial environments.

This process — you probably know it as "management by objective" — largely is what makes IR a profession. It certainly is where the lion's share of the work resides.

A brief example illustrates this best. Some years back, a company was investing heavily in a multimedia attempt to influence a single audience in a single location: financial analysts in New York City.

The company was a profitable operation; the numbers were, if not overwhelming, at least respectable for a corporation with the business mix and market share the company had. Still, management considered the stock undervalued by the investment community, which at that point was looking askance at companies primarily involved in basic manufacturing. Such companies, according to the prevailing wisdom on Wall Street, were too "mature" and managerially too staid to compete with the new stars, the financial and service-oriented companies.

And that, of course, was the rub. The "quest for excellence" fad was raging at the time, and in the absence of an effective vaccine, the chairman had come down with a bad case of it.

His case manifested itself in all the classic symptoms: He sent top managers to Outward Bound, hoping the survivors would bring back something more substantial than frostbite and lingering fears of peer-group cannibalism; he hired outside experts whose prescriptions always seemed to center on *bushido* and the need to instil a sense of ancestor-worship in the work force. Acting upon the advice of another consultant, he instituted a "management by wandering around" practice, thus creating a palpable sense of paranoia among the lower ranks.

All this created change in the organization, and some of it even brought some improvement. But even after all this *Sturm und Drang,* the effect on the Big Apple analysts (and hence, the stock price) was...zilch.

Why? All this activity was designed to send a message, and did. But it was the wrong message, sent to the wrong audiences. Despite protests to the contrary, the investment community is far less interested in the organizational or cultural aspects of a company than it is concerned with the dollars and cents. Internally, the messages being sent — messages involving, respectively, the need for teamwork, the benefits of shared corporate beliefs and values, and a de- emphasis of hierarchical stratification — may well have been valuable. But to an audience as bottom-line-oriented as the analysts, those messages were virtually irrelevant.

It was not until a savvy IR manager proposed a new set of messages — messages that focused on the protection from cyclical earnings swings that the service/manufacturing diversification offered — that the intended audience began to take notice.

Suddenly, both sides were talking in the same language.

MEDIA

Considering today's wide variety of media — everything from print to TV to electronic bulletin boards — it would seem that the toughest media decision facing the IR manager would be to decide how much money is in the budget and how to go for the biggest bang.

Alas, it is not the case. Mundane fiscal considerations are always one concern in this vale of tears, but the IR manager would be well advised to cry instead over the hard work involved in matching message and audience to the most effective media.

There are headaches aplenty. Sometimes the pain is because the medium becomes, in the words of the prophet of pop communications, the message. Translated, this annoying cliché means the audience will base part of its perceptions on the unspoken messages we send. For a grossly oversimplified example, if one message we want to send is that of elegant prosperity, it ill behooves us to produce an annual report on stock reminiscent of a brown paper bag. Similarly, with few exceptions, serving up hot dogs on paper plates probably sends the wrong message to the *Fortune* reporter researching that article on your company's projected earnings increase. In cases that involve using the medium to send an image message, common sense is your best guide.

But more often, the difficulty arises from a failure of the IR manager to understand that each medium has a set of strengths and weaknesses that must be exploited and avoided, respectively.

Nothing matches the potential impact of video, for example. It literally has the power to knock the socks off the viewer — and that is a strength indeed.

But the weaknesses abound. Video must be simple; a complicated message goes right past the audience. Remember Walter Cronkite trying to explain Watergate with flipcharts? Video must be visual; try holding audience attention with a static, talking-head approach. Video communicates in real time; joy-sticking in fast-forward guarantees loss of message effectiveness. Video requires some relatively inflexible hardware support; try folding up the VCR and television monitor to read on the bus ride home. Video can be — and is usually perceived as being — expensive to produce; using it to send, for instance, a cost-reduction message can be awkward at best.

The point is not to knock video as a vehicle. Rather, it is that *every* available medium has its own particular strengths and weaknesses, and the wise IR practitioner analyzes each project in terms of the most effective medium.

Depending on your budget, and the availability of quality suppliers, producers, printers, and so on, the specifics of your own media strength/weakness analysis will vary. But a few general concepts apply.

Time is usually the most important variable, mainly because of the technical limitations of production. If the need is to distribute information quickly, much of the "sophisticated" media is automatically ruled out: a typewriter-produced news release is more likely to be used than is a slick-looking, typeset publication (though innovations such as desk-top publishing are providing the IR director more options today).

Needed detail is a factor in media decisions. As noted, some media (like video) cannot effectively communicate a lot of detail. In such cases, the communicator usually opts for printed materials, which the reader can scan quickly, skim for important details, and repeatedly refer to at need.

Audience size/location/availability are all factors, especially when the IR functionary sees a need for the presence of a company officer. Most people prefer to receive information from a known authority figure, speaking face-to-face. Message credibility and believability is demonstrably higher when a human being, live and in person, is the source. The impact of the meeting has the same potential impact as any media, plus the cachet of live flesh. Most of video's weaknesses also apply, however, including the potential for visual boredom and the inability to communicate a lot of detail.

The list goes on and on, and once more the IR professional is best served by liberal application of good sense. For instance, logic tells us that a combination of two or more of these media — say, a press conference at which supporting, printed materials are also provided — would provide a more effective, cumulative delivery than either medium alone.

And, fortunately, common sense ratifies my final observation: The three essential elements we've discussed — audience, message, and media — are interdependent. None can be considered effective in the absence of the other two.

The IR function is, above all, a function that must be *managed*, in every sense of the word. Management must include development of a cohesive strategy, based upon the strategic plan of the corporation the IR function serves. The strategy must go beyond the surface and anticipate the audience's interest, message interpretation, and ultimate reaction. The IR practitioner must understand the technical limitations of each available medium and know what messages are being sent merely by the choice of medium.

And when all these elements come together in the planned harmony of an effective IR program, the IR manager finds himself or herself in an enviable position — that of the consummate professional who understands the task at hand, knows what actions to apply, and is acknowledged by the organization as producing, and being, something of value.

* * * * *

Earl Merkel is president of Earl Merkel Communications Group, a privately held firm that counsels several Fortune 500 corporations about unifying marketing, media, and communications presentations in consolidated programs for internal and external audiences.

CREATING EFFECTIVE RELATIONSHIPS WITH SECURITIES ANALYSTS

Olha Holoyda

Although securities analysts and corporate officials have the same goal of reaching the investing public with company information, at times the relationship may be adversarial. Corporate officials, particularly if new to dealing with analysts, naturally seek to present their company in the best possible light. In doing so, company officers may approach analysts with some trepidation, seeing them as necessary evils, suspicious individuals with the power to influence the price of the company's stock — favorably as well as adversely. Analysts, on the other hand, consider their mission to be the objective analysis of all facets of a company's operations — from the CEO's personality and future vision of company development to the efficiency of manufacturing operations.

Underlying fundamentals and attendant analyses are important, of course, as the analyst develops an understanding about the company and a relationship with management. Corporations will go through cycles — both long- and short-lived, positive and negative. The single most important factor in an analyst's as well as in Wall Street's perception of management at any time is credibility.

THE CREDIBILITY FACTOR

In good, but especially in bad times, whether it be the first or the tenth in a series of follow-up meetings, management credibility takes precedence over all other fundamental factors. Even a single slip in forthrightness can haunt a corporation for a long time. Wall Street tends to be extremely unforgiving when negative surprises occur.

Periodic updates and changes in corporate strategic plans should be communicated as soon as practicable. Inevitably a company will stumble, reporting a bad quarter or half or year for reasons ranging from a defective product recall to outside, industrywide influences. A common mistake among fledgling companies — particularly highly visible ones — is the attempt by management to evade bad news and its consequences for as long as possible by claiming that the quarter will hold no surprises when in actuality the situation is quite the reverse.

Analysts respect company management that bites the bullet and announces bad news early. Although the stock may perform negatively in immediate response to the news, over the longer term management has earned credibility. Often, in fact, if the Street has been made aware of an upcoming difficult period, the price may not change because shareholders consider management's statements to be a fair representation of the situation. Institutional and individual investors may decide to remain holders through the near-term rough spot upon review of solid long-term performance by existing management.

In attempts to make their story better known among analysts and investors and, consequently, boost the stock price, companies often arrange "dog and pony" shows. If credibility becomes an issue, these efforts can backfire. After the initial meeting with about 50 analysts in New York City, the management of a health care company saw its stock decline by almost 13 percent. Why? Analysts left the meeting with the impression management was glossing over problems by not responding to questions about a new product that had exhibited problems upon installation and customer usage. Although no negative news had been announced, analysts perceived — and correctly so — that all the glitches in the product had not been remedied. Other examples of corporate unresponsiveness may be due to fear of losing a competitive advantage, to the lack of preparation, or to unwillingness to relate a change in strategy because of the possibility of failure. Such reasoning tends to be regarded as weak by analysts.

BASIC INFORMATIONAL REQUIREMENTS AND THE SYNTHESIS

Analysts' basic sources of company information are past and latest annual reports, 10-Ks, quarterly statements, 10-Qs, proxy statements, and press releases. Some companies provide published reports from brokerage firms, newspaper and magazine articles, relevant trade publications, and profile summaries compiled by IR professionals. The detail varies. One major drug store chain provides analysts with quarterly margin statistics dating back five years, comparable store sales on a monthly basis, and a quarterly store count summary in addition to standard data. A large food processor sends along a chatty, glossy-magazine-type quarterly that includes consumer comments and recipes featuring its products as main ingredients. At the other extreme are bare-bones financial statements that contain a sparse management commentary.

Obviously the analyst's preference is for as much relevant data as possible and as much management commentary as necessary to determine how well — or poorly — the fiscal year is progressing as compared with previously stated objectives. (Glossy covers and breathtaking photos can't hide deteriorating fundamentals.)

A good analyst will digest the entire informational packet sent by the company. Among other factors, historical trends and potential future growth rates, financial ratios, balance-sheet statistics, and comparisons of company objectives with actual achievements will be analyzed.

The analyst may also run industry screens and comparable-company screens to determine rank in terms of sales and earnings growth and profitability, debt utilization, and other appropriate ratios.

THE GENERIC ANALYST

Analysts may be divided into two broad categories: "buy-side" and "sell-side" in Wall Street jargon. A simplistic definition might state that buy-side analysts (working for such customers as pension and mutual funds) purchase stocks based on the recommendation of sell-side analysts (who also typically sells to their firm's retail brokers and their clients). Buy-side analysts rely heavily on purchased research and opinions, but may visit company management as well to form their own recommendations. The buy-side analyst's supervisor, the portfolio manager, makes the decision, either alone or in committee, to include the stock in a managed portfolio. Sell-side analysts, on the other hand, spend most of their time kicking the tires of the company and its management and writing original reports.

Major Wall Street firms can employ extensive research staffs, easily numbering over a hundred, to cover all industry sectors from manufacturing to finance. Regional firms tend to focus more narrowly — on companies in their own backyards, underfollowed situations, or firms fitting some specialized criteria (i.e., emerging growth, contrarian philosophy, low valuations to market).

In determining suitability of coverage, analysts may be restricted by the size of capitalization or the number of shares outstanding. Fund objectives may also have a restrictive effect on buy-side analyst coverage.

Despite the diversity of analyst backgrounds, objectives, and expertise, each analyst is somewhat generic. At some point all will ask the same questions.

A CHECKLIST FOR THE INITIAL MEETING WITH AN ANALYST

The first meeting with a company provides the analyst with one of the most important elements of analysis — the corporate culture as personified by its officers. Even the most ebullient and personable corporate president must be thoroughly prepared. If not willing to delve into each division's profit margin, the CEO should delegate the responsibility and advise the analyst that the subject will be explored with another well-versed officer at a later point.

Analysts' levels of sophistication regarding the industry and company specifics vary. The CEO or spokesperson should attempt to determine the amount of expertise and offer the analyst the option of listening to a short structural outline or starting directly with questions and answers.

As even the best-written financial information cannot provide all details, a guideline checklist for the initial meeting with an analyst is provided below.

General Background: Industry and Company

- Industry climate: infancy, growth, consolidation, maturation stage.
- Company description, definition, industry classification.
- Company's susceptibility to recession, depression, low- and high-growth economic environment.
- Differentiation from others within and outside the defined industry.
- Short history of company's evolution.
- Implications of high and low interest rates, inflation rates.
- Effect of changing demographics, markets, customer demand.
- Impact of global conditions, including foreign competition, currency exchange rates.
- Company strategy and philosophy of top management.
- Strengths and weaknesses from management's viewpoint — past and expected.
- The "worst case" scenario.
- Management structure and responsibility.
- Chain of command: president and key officers, regional and divisional managers, staff.
- Backgrounds of top management officials.
- Direct and indirect competition.
- Regulatory and legislative constraints.
- Company policy in event of takeover bid.
- Acquisition program, candidate profiles, and strategy.
- Divestiture plan, if applicable.
- Suggestion of relevant trade journals, government publications, industry associations for background and trend information.

Company Specifics

- Sales and profit growth history.
- Sustainable long-term expansion plans.
- Importance and contribution of various divisions.
- Market share or rank.
- Unique niche or differentiation, product and/or service offerings.
- Vertical and horizontal integration.
- Contribution of overseas activities and joint ventures.
- Dependence on major suppliers.
- Dependence on major customers.
- If manufacturer, details of operation, tour of plant.
- Computerization, automation, distribution systems and capabilities.
- Sources of raw materials, labor, energy.
- Relationships with labor unions, employees.
- New product introductions.
- In-house and outside design, research, and development capabilities.
- Health of mature products.
- Productivity measurements as compared with industry standards.
- Pricing policies, noncompetitive and competitive markets.
- Advertising and promotional activities.
- Marketing strategies.
- Employee compensation and incentive plans.
- Initial training and continuing education programs.
- Manager, staff turnover.
- Promotion policies.
- Capacity utilization during seasons, cycles.
- Layoff policies.

Financial Structure and Trends

- Margins: gross; selling, general, and administrative; operating; net. Current and expected rates, possible changes and reasons.
- Projected sales, operating and net profits, earnings per share — company estimates or comments on analysts' forecasts.

- Tax rates, proposed legislative changes.
- Asset valuation with focus on inventories, real estate, and cash balances.
- Appropriate ratio analyses: activity, leverage, liquidity, debt coverage/repayment.
- Manufacturing facilities and real estate: ownership and/or leasing policies.
- Inventory valuation, treatment under tax laws.
- Depreciation schedules, impact on financials.
- Inflation-adjusted numbers.
- Cash flow, adequacy, use of excess dollars: acquisitions, dividend increases, stock repurchase programs.
- Available bank lines of credit.
- Accounts receivable payment cycle, industry norm.
- Capital expenditures: five-year plan, financing.
- Research and development, past and future commitments.
- Patents and trademarks, importance and longevity.
- Balance sheet trends, asset and liability relationships.
- Sources and uses of funds.
- Capitalization structure, debt versus equity, comparison to industry norm.
- Debt ratings, reasons for changes.
- Financing, near- and long-term needs. Equity, debt, or a combination.
- Return on assets, net worth, equity goals.
- Statistics relevant to the industry, e.g., in retailing, sales per square foot/store square footage, sales per store/number of stores, comparable (stores open one year or longer) store sales, industry benchmarks.

Shareholder Information

- Price action and reasons, particularly if volatile patterns.
- Price/earnings ratio, premium or discount, rationale and goals; comparison with other firms' and industry average.
- Dividend payment, stock split policies.
- Insider ownership, changes.
- Institutional ownership, changes.
- Significant interested party holding (13-D filings).
- Stock repurchase plans.
- Current analyst coverage, recommendations, estimates.

BUILDING A FOLLOWING ON THE STREET

Generally highly capitalized, NYSE-listed firms have a strong analyst following, as do selected ASE-listed and over-the-counter-traded companies. Analysts have already taken the initiative and regularly visit the covered company and meet with the CEO, CFO, divisional managers, and other key personnel. Periodic telephone calls supplement the personal appointments.

Underfollowed companies have a choice of various methods to gain the Street's attention. The best way to ensure an audience is to offer a good story. Analysts — particularly those concentrating on regional, special situation, or emerging growth areas — spend a lot of time sifting through screens and annual reports in search of their next possible winning stock. Obviously, if analysts engaged in providing institutional-type coverage are targeted, a wider audience is reached. However, some firms may prefer to expand the amount of shares held in individual investors' portfolios.

Access to analysts may be gained directly or indirectly. The most time-effective manner is the breakfast or luncheon meeting, hosted by a local analysts' or stockbrokers' society and preceded by a mailing of informational packets. Initial meetings should be held in or near corporate headquarters — as a dress rehearsal — and where the reception should be warmest. The larger investment communities in which concentrations of analysts and portfolio managers work should be targeted next. Usually such meetings are arranged by professional IR firms, which direct management through a series of meetings over several weeks.

Some companies target specific analysts and initiate meetings on a one-to-one basis. This tactic should probably be minimized.

If the budget does not allow for direct contact through analyst or broker society meetings, an alternative is the focused mailing. Mailing lists compiled according to analyst specialty are available through analyst societies or companies specializing in tailored mailing lists. Such a mailing should include a letter of introduction by the corporate spokesperson highlighting appropriate facts, an annual and a 10-K report, the quarterly statements, and pertinent press releases. A follow-up phone call would also be in order.

Appropriate financial and local newspapers and periodicals should be recipients of regular mailings addressed to the editor. This is an indirect way of attracting analysts: A reporter's interest may be spurred to the extent that a story is researched and written about the company.

Last, two common points, while seemingly minor, tend to have a huge impact when ignored: unreturned phone calls and lack of a secondary spokesperson to handle queries when the primary individual is unavailable.

* * * * *

Olha Holoyda has been a securities analyst with several national and regional brokerages and is now researching and writing a two-year investment project in Washington, D.C. She holds an MBA in finance, a JD, a CFA certification, and several securities industry licenses.

CREATING EFFECTIVE RELATIONSHIPS WITH BONDHOLDERS

Martin S. Fridson, CFA
Morgan Stanley & Co. Incorporated

During my years as a fixed-income analyst I have found most IR officers to be competent and responsive to my needs, although frequently uncomprehending of them. To the best of my recollection, I too have conducted myself professionally, even when not welcomed as warmly as I might have wished. At times this has required considerable forbearance. In one instance, I traveled across the continent to meet with an IR manager. He began the interview in his office by questioning my firm's wisdom in paying me a presumably exorbitant salary, since I appeared to him to be duplicating the efforts of a similarly well-heeled equity analyst. He graciously acknowledged, however, that it was really none of his affair whether my firm was spending its money intelligently.

In the same generous spirit, I am willing to grant that IR officers can legitimately question fixed-income analysts' economic value to their companies. Corporations that come to the public debt market infrequently may have particular difficulty in discerning a payback on time spent with bondholders or providers of fixed-income research. Accordingly, it is worthwhile to devote a few paragraphs to explaining the connection between fixed-income analysts' activities and shareholder value. Although not as widely appreciated as the link between equity analysts' efforts and stock prices, the value of communicating effectively with fixed income-analysts is real and substantial.

By enabling a corporation to lock in reduced borrowing costs for as much as 40 years, a well-told fixed-income story can have a far more lasting benefit than a clever concept that causes millions of shares to trade but is forgotten within a few weeks.

BEYOND RATING

Before allowing me to proceed with my argument, the skeptic may interject, "What do fixed-income analysts have to do with borrowing costs? Aren't interest rate differentials among corporations determined by the rating agencies? My company already spends plenty of time trying to get upgraded, so how could analysts possibly help us?"

I can readily understand how an IR officer could form the impression that bond ratings determine borrowing cost differentials, plain and simple. Investment banks and the financial press publish rate schedules that might seem to imply that a double-A industrial, for sake of illustration, is assured of obtain-

EXHIBIT 1
Sample Long-Term Interest Rate Schedule (as of May 18, 1987)

| | Term | | |
Sector	5 Years	10 Years	30 Years
Industrials			
AAA	8.79%	9.27%	9.76%
AA	8.89%	9.40%	10.01%
A	8.99%	9.52%	10.54%
BBB	9.49%	9.74%	10.86%
Electric Utilities			
AAA	8.79%	9.30%	10.01%
AA	8.91%	9.42%	10.11%
A	9.04%	9.57%	10.21%
BBB	9.32%	9.80%	10.71%
Finance Companies			
AAA	8.84%	9.35%	9.91%
AA	8.94%	9.49%	10.16%
A	9.09%	9.62%	10.36%

Source: Morgan Stanley & Co., Incorporated.

ing 10-year money at 9.40 percent, while a triple-B electric utility can expect to borrow for 30 years at 10.71 percent (Exhibit 1). An unsophisticated corporate treasurer might liken these schedules to the non-negotiated admission charges at a movie theater, where those aged 65 and over are entitled to a specified discount and matinees cost precisely so much less than evening shows. Each ticket purchaser can be assigned to a discrete category, and nobody can bargain for a 15- or 25-cent reduction. In contrast, there is necessarily some variation around general rate levels in the bond market, for not every issuer fits neatly into the rating agencies' pigeonholes of triple-A, double-A, and so on.

The most obvious difficulty with pricing debt solely according to ratings is that the rating agencies do not always agree. Considering only the two most widely followed agencies, Moody's and Standard & Poor's, 137 out of a sample of 520 actively traded issuers were in different rating categories (e.g., AAA by Moody's and AA by Standard & Poor's) as of mid-1987. If there were only two agencies to contend with, and if they never differed by more than one category, assigning risk premiums would still not be much more complex than the published schedules imply. Investors could simply price a "split-rated" company's debt midway between the rates shown for its two rating categories. Unfortunately, at least three other agencies (Duff and Phelps, Fitch, and McCarthy, Crisanti & Maffei) also have adherents among investors, so the possible permutations of split ratings are staggering.

Furthermore, the agencies occasionally diverge radically in their perceptions of credit quality. For example, in 1987 Chesebrough-Pond's was rated BAA2 ("medium grade ... neither highly protected nor poorly secured") by Moody's and AAA ("highest rating ... extremely strong") by Standard & Poor's. Beginning in 1982, Moody's rated Hudson's Bay Oil & Gas A, while Standard & Poor's assigned it a speculative-grade rating of BB+. Disparities as wide as these may reflect opposite expectations about the outcome of regulatory proceedings, differing interpretations of informal credit support, or conflicting opinions about legal aspects of a bond indenture. In such cases, it is absurd for the investor to choose an intermediate position; as John Kenneth Galbraith remarked in another context, truth is not the average of right and wrong.

In an effort to come down on one side or the other, the portfolio manager may seek the advice of a fixed-income analyst, either in house or at a brokerage firm. When this happens, the company in question stands the best chance of a favorable decision if it has for some time been telling its story to the individuals who strongly influence the decision maker.

It is not solely when the rating agencies disagree, however, that it pays for a corporation to have established rapport with fixed-income analysts. For many investors, ratings are not the exclusive — nor, in some cases, the primary — determinants of approval for purchase. At some institutions, an in-house research staff (possibly a single analyst) begins with the universe of companies that meet some minimum rating standard (e.g., single-A by least one agency) and eliminates from that list companies that appear vulnerable to downgrading. Sometimes these efforts to be more discriminating than the rating agencies succeed in weeding out credits that subsequently fall to lower ratings. In other cases, though, analysts bar their portfolio managers from buying perfectly sound credits, by either misinterpreting financial data or placing insufficient emphasis on qualitative factors that rating agencies rightly consider.

For example, some pharmaceutical companies have significantly higher debt-to-capital ratios than similarly rated manufacturing companies, yet at this writing their ratings are generally not in jeopardy. The drug producers' debt is largely offset by cash earned and invested in Puerto Rico, which the companies, in order to exploit a special tax benefit, have declined to repatriate. At any time, the companies can pay a "tollgate" tax and bring these funds back to the United States to liquidate their borrowings. Clearly, the pharmaceutical companies' debt creates less financial risk than a capital goods manufacturer's borrowings, proceeds of which are invested in fixed assets and not readily convertible to cash.

To an analyst who has never heard this idiosyncrasy explained by an articulate IR manager, however, the drug company could appear overleveraged. The manager of a billion-dollar fixed-income portfolio might as a consequence be precluded from investing in it, and the corporation's borrowing cost might in turn rise through an unnecessary narrowing of the market for its bonds. For a large and frequent borrower, being eliminated from institutions' approved lists can severely crimp ability to raise funds in the public market at any interest rate. The institutions that continue to buy that borrower's debt may reach their limits on exposure to a single borrower (e.g., 5 percent of assets), preventing them from buying more, even at a higher yield.

These consequences, costly as they may be to the borrower, do not necessarily imply that the institutional fixed-income analyst has been negligent. Rather, the inappropriate credit veto may arise from a heavy work load that, when combined with extremely broad responsibilities (coverage of all industrials, utilities, banks, and finance companies is a common job description at smaller institutions), precludes intimate familiarity with each industry. By the same token, it is equally difficult for a one- or two-person IR department to convey a complex story directly to fixed-income analysts at hundreds of institutions. Communicating periodically with analysts at a handful of investment banks, however, can assure that the company's message will reach thousands of decision makers through these firms' research publications. Investor relations professionals who have not hitherto dealt with bond analysts can get started by writing to:

> President
> Fixed Income Analysts Society, Inc.
> Post Office Box 1025
> New York, NY 10005

FIASI is a professional organization founded in 1977 that includes buy-side, sell-side, and rating agency fixed-income analysts. (Associate membership is open to IR officers.) The organization hosts a series of luncheon meetings, many of which consist of company presentations. Appearing before FIASI can be a cost-effective way of educating the people who directly influence a company's borrowing costs.

The speculative-grade (i.e., rated below BAA3 by Moody's or below BBB– by Standard & Poor's) sector provides an especially vivid illustration of the benefits to a company's borrowing costs of going beyond the annual trip to the rating agencies. High-yield securities (popularly known as "junk bonds") represent a growing but still comparatively inefficient sector of the capital markets.

The primary market for lower-rated bonds began to be sizable only in the late 70s. As a result, the high-yield sector lacks much of the infrastructure, including a large coterie of seasoned analysts, that facilitates efficient pricing of risk in the longer-established high-grade market. Many of the speculative-grade issuers, moreover, have low ratings not because they are financially overextended or failing, but because they are emerging growth companies with relatively high operating risk. In many cases, their capitalization is too small to have attracted extensive institutional equity research coverage, so the portfolio manager has available little third-party (i.e., independent of the issuer and the underwriter) research, and is therefore understandably inclined to err on the side of conservatism. Moody's and Standard & Poor's rate the speculative-grade issues, but their ratings correlate only loosely with market risk premiums. Whereas yields on the best and worst double-A credits may vary by no more than 25 basis points, the single-B category embraces companies that the market sometimes differentiates by a spread of 400. Clearly, a company with this rating has an incentive to persuade investors that it is among the stronger rather than weaker single-B credits.

BOTTOM-LINE BENEFITS

Very well, the reader may say at this point, spending time with fixed income analysts could save my company some money, but are the potential savings material? To answer this question, imagine a company with $500 million of book equity. If the company saves just 10 basis points on a $250 million bond issue, the net income impact (assuming a 34 percent tax rate) is $165,000 annually. At an earnings multiple of 12, this represents an increase of nearly $2 million in shareholder value, not a bad payoff on a side activity for an IR professional concerned primarily with equity analysts.

Even greater benefits can accrue to shareholders if a company can persuade fixed-income investors that its credit quality is not only better than rating agencies believe, but rising as well. Exhibit 2 illustrates, from the investor's viewpoint, the total returns achievable through investing in issues that have potential for upgrading.

In Scenario 1, the bond of a triple-B borrower is purchased at the going rate of 10.86 percent. Its price will appreciate from 100.117 to 102.719 if it is upgraded one year later to single-A. At that point the market will price the bond at a 10.54 percent yield, assuming no change in the general level of interest rates in the interim. Total return for the holding period, which reflects the bond's initial yield and subsequent appreciation, is 13.24 percent.

This is a much better result than can be obtained by simply buying a triple-B bond that remains a triple-B and continues to be priced at a 10.86 percent yield. Total return in that case is identical to the 10.86 percent yield to maturity. The improving credit's advantage (13.24 percent − 10.86 percent = 2.38 percent is so great that if persuaded of the likelihood of upgrading, investors will be willing to accept a yield to maturity of less than 10.86 percent, resulting in a cost savings for the corporation. The reason is that even if purchased at a yield significantly below the prevailing triple-B rate, the bond that is headed for an upgrading can provide investors a higher return than the non-improving triple-B issue.

In Scenario 2, the investor purchases a new issue at a 10.70 percent yield-to-maturity yet realizes an 11.89 percent total return, or roughly 100 basis points more than the expected return on a stable triple-B credit.

Using the same tax and earnings multiple assumptions employed in the preceding example of a 10-basis point savings (page 89), we find that persuading investors of a company's upgrade potential when bringing a $250-million offering to market can raise shareholder value by over $3 million.

These examples, based as they are on total return, may be at variance with some readers' image of fixed-income portfolio management. There was, it is true, a time when income and capital preservation were the sole objectives of most bond managers. Even today, the life insurance industry, one of the dominant participants in the bond market, faces formidable regulatory barriers to completely active management. In contrast, however, pension fund sponsors typically evaluate their fixed-income managers on the basis of total return. Bond mutual funds, too, find themselves in competition with their peers, with the score kept in total return.

In this struggle for interim returns, spotting improving and deteriorating credits is only one available technique (along with market timing, arbitrage swapping, and sector rotation), but many fixed-income managers rely heavily on it. A bond that is not merely stable but improving in quality can be extremely valuable to such managers. Their willingness to pay a premium for that value represents a potential boon to the corporate borrower.

EXHIBIT 2
Expected Return on an Improving Credit
New Borrowing Rate on 30-Year Industrial Bond

Rating	Yield-to-Maturity
A	10.54%
BBB	10.86%

Total Return on Bond Upgraded from BBB to A in One Year

	Coupon	Maturity	Purchase Price (Yield)	Price One Year after Purchase	Total Return
Scenario 1	10 7/8%	30 years	100.117 (10.86%)	102.719 (10.54%)	13.24%
Scenario 2	10 3/4%	30 years	100.405 (10.70%)	101.701 (10.54%)	11.89%

Notes: Bonds are quoted, in accordance with industry practice, in percentage of face amount — i.e., 100 (par) is equivalent to $1,000. Assumed reinvestment rate is the median of the initial yield and ending yield.

The value of being perceived as an improving credit has increased in recent years because of the trend toward more aggressive use of debt financing by corporations. There has been growing pressure from institutional investors (and from take-over artists) to translate corporate resources into immediate enhancement of share prices. Excess debt capacity is commonly viewed as one such resource. Accordingly, many companies have come to believe that they are shortchanging their shareholders if they fail to borrow as much as they prudently can, either to expand their operations or to repurchase equity. Corporations that formerly satisfied all their cash needs from internal sources are now floating bonds and finding they need to develop positive images among fixed-income investors. Other companies, already well-known to bondholders as a result of frequent debt offerings, are now returning to the market with dramatically altered balance sheets. To minimize the resulting rise in their borrowing costs, corporations must demonstrate the ability to service their increased debt burdens. In some cases, the success of a recapitalization may hinge on the IR department's effectiveness in convincing bondholders of the corporation's financial staying power. Such circumstances make it especially worthwhile to understand and meet the fixed-income analyst's needs.

WHAT BOND ANALYSTS WANT

To serve this important but possibly unfamiliar client the corporation should begin by inviting fixed-income specialists to all its analyst group presentations. As discussed below, the fixed-income analyst is no mere number-cruncher who bases credit decisions solely on a company's historical financial ratios. Any good analyst considers the possibility that future ratios may look better (or worse) than past figures and values the forward-looking input that a skilled IR manager can provide.

Assessment of management is likewise an essential part of the fixed-income analyst's job, and one that the analyst can do properly only with access to senior executives. This means not just financial executives, but also operating people and those with ultimate responsibility for a company's strategy. A corporation's written communications, too, should reflect fixed-income analysts' desire for a broad understanding of its business. Like their equity counterparts, fixed-income analysts welcome mailings on new products and market trends. Knowing how a company will generate cash flow in the future is more important than calculating how much it generated last year.

All of this said, IR officers might conclude fixed-income analysts require exactly the same information as the equity analyst. Indeed, as a general rule, it is better to send fixed-income analysts equity-oriented material that may sometimes have marginal value than to assume they do not want it. For example, the most direct effect of dividend policy is on shareholders, yet credit analysts may see in a dividend cut either a prudent cash conservation step or a signal of financial distress. The better informed they are, the more likely they are to interpret dividend actions correctly.

Similarly, a sudden run-up in a company's stock price may reflect accumulation by a hostile raider who plans to finance a takeover mainly with borrowed funds, the result of which will be a severe downgrading of the company's bonds. If there is some other explanation for the run-up, such as a new buy recommendation by a prominent equity analyst, the company should certainly make bond analysts aware of it. By so doing, the company can dispel a cloud that might otherwise hang over its debt and raise its borrowing cost.

Notwithstanding fixed-income and equity analysts' many joint interests, however, at certain points their paths of inquiry diverge. To mention one gross example, equity analysts are concerned with the earning power of publicly owned corporations, some of which are holding companies that issue little public debt, but instead borrow at the operating company level. Fixed-income analysts are more interested than their equity colleagues are in the subsidiaries' financial statements. Equity analysts, moreover, are unlikely to wish to delve into the intricacies of provisions for early redemption of high-coupon bonds. They probably want to know the earnings-per-share impact of retiring expensive debt, but exactly how the corporation accomplishes it has no direct impact on shareholders.

To bondholders, though, it matters a great deal whether the issuer offers to repurchase the bonds at a premium to the market or capitalizes on an indenture provision that permits mandatory redemption at a price below the market. The latter case often arises in connection with electric utility bonds, many of which can be called under special "maintenance and replacement" and "property release" clauses. Debentures of industrial corporations generally have less complicated call provisions.

Nonetheless, an industrial bond's value can change suddenly if the issuer announces a major asset sale or equity offering, events that may trigger a redemption otherwise precluded by a prohibition on retiring debt with the proceeds of new borrowings.

Another topic that is largely irrelevant to the equity analyst but critical to the bond analyst is the legal status of the debt of an acquired company. Although acquisition-related press releases often state the acquirer will "assume" debt of the acquired company, in a legal sense at least three distinct things may happen. First, the acquirer may in fact legally assume the debt, meaning that it becomes the obligor and extinguishes the acquired company's corporate identity. Second, the acquirer may guarantee the debt of the acquired company, which remains the obligor and retains its corporate identity. Finally, the acquired company may continue its separate (but wholly-owned) corporate existence while its debt is neither assumed nor guaranteed by the acquirer. In this case bondholders can look only to implicit support from the new parent. These three distinct outcomes have different implications for bondholders, particularly if the acquirer subsequently divests the subsidiary.

Mastering the arcane details of these subjects is unnecessary for most IR officers. Instead, they should probably encourage the fixed-income analyst to speak directly on such matters to the treasurer or an assistant treasurer, who will immediately understand the questions and ordinarily have little difficulty in obtaining the answers. These individuals may not be accustomed to speaking with analysts, however. If so, the IR officer can facilitate the communication by reassuring them on the disclosure question.

No fixed-income analyst who adheres to ethical standards of practice will ask a treasurer to divulge, prior to a general dissemination, the corporation's intentions with respect to early redemption. The analyst simply wishes to know whether conditions exist that could lead to a call.

For example, the proceeds of a planned divestment may be earmarked for some purpose, previously disclosed, other than debt retirement. Alternately, the fixed-income analyst may seek a general statement of policy. This sort of request is analogous to an equity analyst's inquiry concerning the dividend, made with the knowledge that the official decision to raise, maintain, or cut it will be disclosed in good time. An analyst who wishes to know whether an acquiring company will guarantee a new subsidiary's debt may, for example, ask what the acquiring company has done in the past under similar circumstances.

Also in the policy realm, IR officers should stand prepared to answer general questions regarding the corporation's attitude toward financial risk and bond ratings. Is the present ratio of debt to capital at the top or the bottom of the range with which the board of directors feels comfortable? Does the company consider maintenance of its present ratings a cornerstone of its corporate philosophy, or do other objectives take precedence? A corporation cannot guarantee to bondholders that its ratings will remain constant; not even the rating agencies can make that assurance. Still, the fixed-income analyst can make more intelligent judgments by at least knowing what level of credit quality the corporation is shooting for.

Besides asking companies questions that never come up in discussions with equity analysts, fixed-income analysts also have specialized interests in the area of financial reporting. By failing to consider the fixed-income perspective on reporting, the corporation may omit optional disclosures that are valuable to, and enhance its standing with, an important constituency.

For example, a few corporations still report interest expense only net of interest income. Whatever benefit a company believes it derives from keeping the gross figure confidential must be weighed against the difficulty consequently posed to fixed-income analysts. Reporting interest expense on a net basis prevents the analyst from directly comparing the company with its peers on the key ratio of fixed charge coverage. Given their duty to be conservative, analysts may assume that interest income is higher (and fixed charge coverage therefore lower) than in reality. Granted, a corporation that perennially maintains a large portfolio of marketable securities looks worse than it ought to in a coverage comparison with companies that generate negligible interest income. Rather than using this argument to justify reporting interest expense on a net basis, however, the company is better off showing the gross figure on its income statement and instructing its IR department to explain the mitigating circumstances to fixed-income analysts. Bond specialists are sophisticated enough to understand the argument and will recognize that the liquidity afforded by a large and permanent securities portfolio offsets the low coverage ratio.

Similarly, fixed-income analysts are capable of adjusting for seasonal borrowings, so there is no need to hide such debt by lumping it, as some companies do in their interim statements, with accounts payable in a single current liabilities account. Breaking out short-term debt in quarterly reports demonstrates genuine consideration for fixed-income investors' needs. Corporations that wish to be even more considerate might adopt the laudable practice, currently followed by only a few companies, of reporting capitalized interest on a quarterly basis.

SOME POPULAR MISCONCEPTIONS

In the same spirit of storing up the goodwill of fixed-income analysts against a time when the corporation may need it, IR officers would do well to discard some popular misconceptions about bond research.

Misconception One: Bond Analysis Is Purely Quantitative

This pervasive belief, although reinforced by whatever personal experience most people have had with credit analysis, is totally mistaken. I have observed some equity analysts registering astonishment upon confronting bond analysts from their own firms at company presentations. "Why do you want to meet management?" they ask in genuine bewilderment. "The company's debt ratio is low, so there can be no question about creditworthiness."

The equity analysts' surprise is only natural, however, considering the inferences they are likely to have drawn from their own experiences in applying for credit. Typically, an application for a credit card or charge account is completely impersonal and determined solely by the numbers — salary, years in present job, amount of debt outstanding. Financial textbooks perpetuate the cut-and-dried image of credit analysis by detailing the ratios used as a framework by bond analysts, while conveying little of the subjective element that goes into the final credit judgment. In today's environment, a company's present financial leverage may be far less important than its perceived ability to adapt to change before its cash flow begins to suffer.

Finally, awareness of the sophisticated quantitative techniques used in other aspects of bond investment, such as management of interest rate risk, undoubtedly rubs off on credit research, lending it a highly numbers-oriented image. Overcoming all this misleading evidence and understanding, as bond analysts do, that a corporation's competitive vigor is ultimately more important than its historical financial ratios, is an essential step toward establishing effective IR with the fixed-income world.

Misconception Two: The Fixed-Income Analyst Is a Research Assistant to the "Real" (i.e., Equity) Analyst

The IR manager of an industrial corporation may speak to the equity research specialist at a brokerage firm or major institution daily. Typically quite specialized in their industry coverage and sensitive to minor fluctuations in earnings prospects, equity analysts spend a large portion of their time on the telephone with the IR officers of a handful of companies. In the process they become quite well known to those individuals. In contrast, it is feasible for a fixed-income analyst to cover a rather large universe of high-grade industrials. Many of the companies the analyst covers have debt that trades infrequently and earnings that ordinarily remain within a narrow enough range to preclude serious risk of downgrading. In such cases, an occasional maintenance-style review suffices to keep the bond analyst current. Less frequent contact naturally results in a less intimate relationship with the IR officer than the equity analyst enjoys.

Unless the IR officer expressly wishes to antagonize the fixed-income analyst, however, it is best not to assume that he or she is an underling of the equity analyst. I know of no brokerage firm research effort organized in such a way that fixed-income industry specialists report to corresponding equity analysts. I know of several fixed-income analysts, however, who are partners in their firms, while their equity counterparts, although perhaps better known to the IR community, rank two or three titles lower. If a corporation perceives that some value is provided by fixed-income analysts, its IR officer should refrain from such provocations as neglecting to return their calls on the theory that they will hear anything they need to know from their overlords in the equity research department.

Misconception Three: All Fixed-Income Analysts Cover Electric Utilities

Unlike some of their peers in the industrial sector, most electric utility IR people are accustomed to hearing regularly from fixed-income analysts. Because it is also true that electric utility bonds comprise a large portion (roughly 25 percent) of the total corporate debt market, many utilities' IR departments appear to have concluded that all fixed-income analysts follow the electric industry. Proceeding on this mistaken notion, they go through directories of securities analysts, adding to their mailing lists all names designated as bond specialists. This creates a problem only in that it clutters up the in boxes of fixed-income analysts who cover industrial or finance companies. Nonutility fixed-income analysts will appreciate the courtesy of being deleted from utilities' mailing lists when they so request. The utilities will in turn save their ratepayers and shareholders the postage expense on annuals, quarterlies, and press releases that go straight into analysts' wastebaskets. (In a similar vein, fixed-income analysts will be grateful to be excused from receiving the missives of penny-stock mining companies that have no public debt outstanding yet mail their financial statements to the entire Financial Analysts Federation directory of analysts.)

CONCLUSION

I hope that I have not presented too bleak a picture of the state of relations between corporations and fixed-income analysts. Most IR people to whom I speak are cordial and well-intentioned, if not always perfectly attuned to bondholders' special concerns. A few do a superb job, taking pains to familiarize themselves with the fundamentals of ratings and the mechanics of early redemption. Some speculative-grade companies even roll out the red carpet for fixed-income analysts, viewing them as valuable emissaries to institutional investors who may, after becoming familiar with their debt, consider buying their stock as well. I applaud these exceptions, but in offering these observations I am more eager to reach the currently less-enlightened members of the investor relations profession. If they begin to appreciate the substantial economic benefits of telling their story to fixed-income investors, they may be motivated to learn how to serve this group more effectively. Corporations communicate with their shareholders, when all is said and done, to minimize their cost of capital. I hope that one day every IR officer will consider it an essential part of the job to satisfy the needs of debt-holders, who supply over 40 percent of that capital to nonfinancial corporations in the United States.

* * * * *

Martin S. Fridson is a principal and manager of credit research for Morgan Stanley & Co., Inc. He is a prominent writer on the subject of income investments and credit analysis.

CREATING EFFECTIVE RELATIONSHIPS WITH THE FINANCIAL MEDIA

Beatrice E. Garcia
The Wall Street Journal

The demands on IR practitioners are likely to increase dramatically as they strive to establish effective relationships with the financial media. One reason is that the media's coverage of business has increased dramatically in the last decade. Also business has taken on greater importance in the daily lives of most Americans.

The public's growing interest in business and the economy is demanding an ever-increasing amount of detail from the financial media. If reporters and producers don't have access to information about a company from the firm itself, no matter how much they strive to present an accurate picture, the result will still be one-sided because all aspects of the story won't be aired.

"Of all the creatures in the financial jungle, none is quite so dangerous as a financial journalist coming up on his or her deadline without your company's side of the story," says Tim Metz, a reporter at *The Wall Street Journal*. Having covered mergers and acquisitions for the paper for more than five years, he knows what a critical difference a news story can make in shaping shareholder opinions when there's partial or, worse yet, no comment from the companies involved in a takeover battle.

Supplying the detail and understanding of a corporation that the financial media are after these days is probably best done by IR professionals. In the corporate hierarchy, few other officials aside from the top financial officers know the ins and outs of a company and have access to the executive suite that the financial journalists are looking for. Yet, most IR personnel remain unknown to the financial press, and many are still unwilling to be news sources. However, the financial media should be added to the various constituencies served by IR professionals.

Many IR practitioners believe it's preferable to court Wall Street analysts and big portfolio managers rather than the press. But when it comes to news about a company, chances are that shareholders as well as corporate executives and investment professionals will get it first from a newspaper or from television or radio. If a reporter can't get a company's side of a story, several accidents can happen — the least of which can be a costly slide in the company's stock price.

The oil crisis of the 70s and the raging double-digit inflation that accompanied it, fluctuations in the U.S. dollar, the flooding of U.S. markets with cheap imports, the decline in U.S. manufacturing competitiveness, and the wave of corporate mergers and restructurings in the 80s have made many individuals realize that economic and financial matters can impact Main Street as much as Wall Street. The political environment of the 80s shaped by the Reagan administration's free-enterprise policies, has also helped raise the public's awareness of business.

As interest in business news has grown, so has the financial media. No longer is business reporting just a few lines about yesterday's stock market activity and lightly rewritten press releases handed out by corporations. The competition among the various media to cover business is intense. Newspapers and weekly news magazines have expanded their coverage by adding more pages, employing more staff, and developing special sections.

Television, has also jumped on the bandwagon, especially through the growth of cable networks in the last few years. Today, two of the three major networks have weekly business news programs, and one is experimenting with a daily show. There are about 13 televised business and financial news programs, including the oldest and widely watched "Wall Street Week" with Louis Rukeyser, carried on the Public Broadcasting System. This show is now in its 16th year.

Along with the additional attention devoted to financial matters by television and national publications, business coverage has also become somewhat more fragmented and specialized. Trade publications and magazines covering specific industries are burgeoning. There's also a growing crop of regional magazines covering local city and state businesses, trends, and issues.

As coverage of business news has increased in the last decade, financial reporters themselves have also changed dramatically. A veteran New York City financial writer recalls that in the 40s and 50s the *New York Times* would often let award-winning foreign correspondents, who were now too old to crisscross the globe, mark time until retirement on the business desk, where the work wasn't too tiring or terribly exciting. The business desk was also a haven for eager young beginners who were willing to write business stories as long as they got a chance to work as journalists. But most had hopes of moving on to the city desk or a foreign assignment.

Today, all that has changed. The business desk is no longer the place for beginners to cut their teeth. Some of today's younger crop of reporters actually focused on a career in financial journalism. Many earn their stripes at local daily papers before moving to major business publications. Both the *New York Times* and *The Wall Street Journal* often hire experienced reporters and specialists such as lawyers to cover various aspects of business.

Still there's a crop of young financial journalists, many in their early 20s. In their instances, natural talent and eagerness to work has helped them overcome their lack of experience and attain influential reporting positions early in their careers. But as Dean Rotbart, editor of *The Journalist & Financial Reporting* newsletter, points out, many of these younger journalists are in way over their heads. They learn on the job, often at the expense of their readers and those companies and executives they write about.

All reporters today, both the experienced and the young Turks, know that they must go beyond the earnings releases or the annual meeting proxy statements to get their arms around the companies they are following.

The *Journal's* Tim Metz argues that the task of supplying

the detail and the depth reporters are looking for these days should fall on the shoulders of the IR officer. As he says, "The chief executive officer rarely has more than a few minutes to spare; the chief financial officer can understand the accounting, but might break out in hives at the mere thought of a press interview; and the press relations officer is a financial illiterate who thinks balance sheets are erotic aids for water beds."

While Mr. Metz might be a little hard on the public relations profession, his advice is sensible. He tells young reporters to sidle up to IR officers because they have a good grasp of a company's financial prospects, they understand the numbers, and they already speak for their companies to the professional investment community.

The secret of establishing good relationships with the press hardly requires an advanced degree in rocket science or psychology. But it has a great deal to do with common sense.

The financial press basically works with the same information that Wall Street analysts need to do their jobs. But unlike analysts, many reporters don't have the luxury of following just a few companies or industries. For instance, in a major metropolitan area such as New York, a business reporter may be required to write about earnings declines at money center banks that boosted their loan-loss reserves to cover troubled Third World debt as well as the leveraged buyout of the retailer, R.H. Macy's Co., and the break-up of telecommunications giant American Telephone and Telegraph.

Most business reporters work under intense deadline pressure. Often, reporters have only a few hours to learn the details of complicated corporate developments and be able to explain to readers and viewers how significant these developments are and how they might effect a firm's future. When dealing with a company, reporters want a speedy response to their questions. To explain the details found in earnings statements, financial reports, and proxy statements, reporters want access to a corporate official with enough understanding of a company's workings to put the numbers in perspective. This is where the IR professional can help .

On major developments such as a merger or major acquisition, reporters also want access to top management to explain the company's side of the story.

Openness and candor also go a long way in establishing a good relationship with press as well as shareholders. Since stock price movements are often predicated by investors' and analysts' expectations about a company's future prospects, stock investors hate nothing more than surprises that spoil expectations. And they usually don't take kindly to surprises even if the news is good!

"Companies that regularly share their hopes and expectations with securities analysts and portfolio managers reap tangible results," says Theodore Pincus, chairman of Financial Relations Board, Inc., the nation's largest financial public relations firm. He believes the stock market puts higher values on companies that are candid when talking to the press, analysts, and shareholders.

In an article for *Fortune* magazine in 1986, Mr. Pincus cited Walter B. Kissinger, the chief executive of the Allen Group, an auto replacement parts company in Long Island, New York. Mr. Kissinger routinely shares the company's growth strategy for each business segment and updates his forecasts on how each operation will perform in press interviews and at analyst meetings. The company's measures on return on equity and earnings growth are about average in a group of 41 auto parts makers. But its PE ratio in recent years put the Allen Group among the top 10 companies in this group.

John Cox, senior vice president in charge of corporate communications at Avon Products, Inc., says when top management sees business plans "getting off the norm, the best thing is to say something."

In the Fall 1986, Avon warned investors and analysts when it became clear just how much growth at its Foster Home Health Care unit was slowing because of changes in several government regulations and insurance programs. Avon president John S. Chamberlin outlined the problem and the steps the company planned to take to deal with the changes and revive revenue and profit growth at the health-care unit. Avon's stock price slid more than two points in the days following the news, but then it stabilized and started moving higher in the first quarter of 1987.

Avon's chairman, Hicks B. Waldron, says "We've learned to position company news, good or bad, before a reporter or an analyst, a consumer, or a disgruntled employee does it for us."

The best example of candor and openness is probably Johnson and Johnson's reaction to Tylenol poisonings in the United States in 1982 and again in 1986. The tampering incidents could have been disastrous to J&J. But on both occasions the company took strong and immediate action, accomplishing great comebacks.

The pharmaceutical and personal-care products concern, based in New Brunswick, New Jersey, recalled all its Tylenol capsules, made its top executives available to the press, and put its chairman in commercials to assure the public that it put consumer welfare ahead of everything else.

J&J's stock plunged each time the Tylenol tamperings were the stuff of front-page headlines or led off the six o'clock TV news. But the share price quickly recovered, and Wall Street analysts even recommended buying the shares after the company announced that it had finally decided to discontinue manufacturing all capsules. About a year after the last tamperings were reported, J&J's stock price had risen nearly 50 percent from the level where it stood than before the horrible news broke.

Gerber Products action after glass fragments were found in some of its baby food products in early 1986 wasn't nearly as forceful. It investigated all complaints, but it refused to recall the products and said changing its packaging wasn't practical.

Hand in hand with openness and candor must go credibility. Sugarcoating bad news may fool shareholders and the press once and even twice, but the truth will eventually get out.

Everett Groseclose has had the unique experience of sitting on both sides of the table. First a reporter and editor for *The Wall Street Journal,* he later handled investor relations for Dow Jones and Company for four years. Since 1985 he has been serving as the managing editor of Dow Jones News Service; frequently referred to on Wall Street as "the ticker," the Service is a news wire specializing in corporate news of interest to the equity market.

"Company responsiveness is the most important ingredient to getting fair coverage," he says. Some companies are under the mistaken notion that by refusing to answer a reporter's questions, they will make him or her drop a story. Yet, often that decision is far beyond a reporter's control.

Mr. Groseclose points out that if there's news about a company, especially if it's having an impact on its stock, such news "is legitimately worth our attention."

Most company executives don't mind spending a half hour with a reporter from a local paper or a national business magazine when there's good news to discuss. But if they believe a news story might focus on a negative aspect of their company, these same officials aren't available for comment.

In an April 10, 1987, article in the *New York Times,* Bic Corporation refused to comment on allegations regarding the safety of its disposable butane lighters. The article, by Tamar Lewin, said the company was facing mounting lawsuits on behalf of people who had been burned and in some cases killed by fires allegedly caused by defects in Bic lighters.

The article, based on extensive data culled from lawsuits, estimated that as many as 1,000 lawsuits might have been filed against Bic and that perhaps as many as 3 million lighters malfunction each year. Although Ms. Lewin made several efforts to contact various Bic executives, the only response she got was a lengthy prepared statement.

Perhaps if the company had answered the article's allegations with its own data on the number of lawsuits and malfunctions, the stock market's reaction on the day the story appeared might have been less severe. Bic stock dropped $8, or 25 percent, to $24.625 on the NYSE. Trading in Bic shares was halted for most of the day because of an order imbalance as investors rushed to sell and brokers couldn't find many buyers for the unwanted shares.

Only after the story was published did the company respond. But Bic only made public the lengthy statement that it had previously given to Ms. Lewin.

What kind of information does a financial reporter need?

As observed earlier, a financial journalist is basically working with the same information that a Wall Street analyst might use when following the same firm or industry. But their points of view are usually the opposite. Analysts are looking for information that will produce good investment ideas. Reporters are looking for details that make exciting news stories.

Often, journalists are looking for a sense of how honest companies are in running their businesses. "We cover companies the way we do because members of the public are investing in them," says Albert Scardino, now a real estate reporter for the *New York Times* and winner of 1984 Pulitzer Prize for editorial writing while editor of the *Georgia Gazette,* a weekly paper he and his wife began in 1978.

The basic document about a corporation is its annual report. During the year, a company's quarterly earnings statement gives a picture of how well or poorly a business is running.

Besides getting a sense of a company's strengths and weaknesses, the annual report also provides a quick summary of the firm's operations and gives a listing of its board of directors. These are handy references for future stories.

Good journalists go over an annual report selectively but carefully. Usually they skip the pretty color photographs of the new plant or the new face cream and turn immediately to the accountant's letter to see if it has been qualified or not. That is, they want to see if the company's accountant agreed with all the data in the annual report — if the data gives a truthful representation of a firm's financial health. If an accountant qualifies the report, a reporter with a good nose for news begins to smell a story.

The footnotes that accompany the balance sheet and income statements usually provide interesting reading material for journalists. One editor at *The Wall Street Journal* says that the length of the footnotes "is inversely related to the health of a company." If the business is running well, the footnotes are short. But "If they are long, there may be a story there," he adds.

Yet, the time it takes to shift through the financial minutiae is rarely wasted. Back in 1983, while still at the *Georgia Gazette* in Savannah, Mr. Scardino recalls he got an anonymous tip that Gulfstream Aerospace Corporation, now a division of Chrysler Corporation, was understating its inventories and therefore paying lower county taxes than it should. He was later able to verify the tip through the company's annual and quarterly reports, when Gulfstream started to break out its inventories separately in an attempt to impress potential investors with the strength of its balance sheets.

It was the county tax man who was impressed with the numbers, however, and he reassessed the company's tax bill. After some initial opposition, Gulfstream eventually agreed to the full higher assessment before the story moved beyond Mr. Scardino's local weekly paper and hit the national media.

Much of this extra revenue for the county ended up in the school system's budget, Mr. Scardino recalls. He says the results were ironic because then Gulfstream chairman Allen Paulson was "a chronic complainer about the quality of the local school system, saying it didn't turn out people who were capable of working in his high-tech industry."

Business reporters also work with various documents that corporations must file with the SEC periodically. These include:

- *10-Ks,* which are expanded annual reports that provide other details of a company's dealings, such as its transaction with members of management.
- *Proxy Statements,* which provide information on top executives' salaries and new proposals facing the board of directors.
- *Ownership documents such as Form 13D, 3, and 4,* which show when institutional investors have bought a stake of more than 5 percent in a company and when they increase that stake. These documents also show when corporate insiders — management and directors — are selling their shares or buying more.

Reporters also routinely check the courts, both federal and local, to see if any of the companies they follow are involved in lawsuits. They will periodically check in with a variety of state and federal agencies such as tax and bankruptcy courts.

All these documents are filed at a company's discretion, but they should be made available immediately to the media. It's easiest for reporters to obtain them directly from a company, and since enterprising journalists will get their hands on them anyway, there's no point in not making them available.

Ideally, companies should get all potentially market-affecting information into the hands of the financial press as well as Wall Street analysts as quickly as possible. Most of this information is pretty routine stuff: earnings statements; dividend rate changes; announcements on new products, new marketing, and corporate financing plans such as the sale of new common stock; and changes in management. Undoubtedly, the financial press and investors want to hear any and all details about a potential major change in the ownership of the company, such as a merger offer or leveraged buyout proposal.

Sometimes news that seems far removed from a company's financial prospects, such as the health of a key executive, can have a massive impact on its stock. A corporate officer may feel he would like to keep some medical details out of the public domain, but in many cases, shareholders believe they have a right to know everything about a company. In July 1987, the stock of MCA, Inc., jumped several points in active trading when its chief executive and chairman Lew Wasserman, 73, was rumored to be seriously ill and even dead.

MCA, the giant entertainment company, has been long considered Hollywood's last great asset play, rich in real estate, keeper of some 3,000 films and televisions shows in its vaults, and operator of a half-dozen entertainment-related companies. Some speculators were betting that without Mr. Wasserman at the helm, his heirs might sell his 15 percent stake and put the company on the block.

The surge in MCA's stock was exaggerated by the company's slowness in giving out details of Mr. Wasserman's illness — he was hospitalized to have polyps removed from his intestines and was recuperating nicely.

At least several times a year, there's a fast run-up in Occidental Petroleum's stock because of rumors surrounding the health of Dr. Armand Hammer, its 89-year-old CEO. Some Wall Streeters see undervalued assets just ripe for the picking when they look at this oil company.

How to get along with the financial press?

As readers demand more information from the press and media coverage becomes more fragmented to meet this demand, corporate executives should make a point of getting to know the primary reporters who cover their companies. Courting the hometown newspapers and television stations could be as rewarding as any time spent with an eager reporter from *Fortune* or a producer from CBS television.

Remember that most reporters are following several industries at one time. Alerting reporters about a corporate development or a pending news release that they might be interested in can go a long way in making sure that a company gets media coverage. While there's a danger of going overboard with this technique, Dow Jones' Mr. Groseclose says "If done properly, it can work to the advantage of both the reporter and the company."

Mr. Rotbart of *"The Journalist & Financial Reporting Newsletter"* agrees. He believes that one of the best ways of establishing good contacts with the media is to work with reporters on feature stories, when there isn't a deadline looming or a company crisis at hand. One way to do this, he says, is for IR professionals to research the publications to find out what kinds of stories they are interested in and then offer up story ideas, such as ones that cover industry developments and just aren't in a company's self-interest.

He claims that once a working relationship has developed between the media and a company, most reporters will make sure that when a negative story needs to be done, the bad news is well-documented and the company's point of view aired.

"If a reporter can call the investor relations executive by his or her first name, that kind of relationship can work in a company's favor when things get rough — if only in forcing the reporter to listen more carefully to the company's side of the story," Mr. Rotbart observes. He maintains that once a company has issued a no-comment statement, most reporters aren't likely to go out of their way to tell the firm's side of the story.

Consistency also helps. One newswire editor says while some companies are very diligent about getting earnings and dividend releases to reporters promptly, "they forget to send out word on new marketing plans which are the wave of their futures."

Most IR practitioners know their companies well enough to realize that for reporters to target them as special sources at least makes cursory sense. In smaller companies, a treasurer or chief financial officer may do double duty as the IR officer.

Some of the larger corporations have both an IR officer to deal with Wall Street brokers, analysts, and shareholders and a public relations executive to work with the media. Since both officials are dedicated to raising the public's awareness of their companies, they shouldn't be working at cross purposes. But sadly, they often do.

It's essential that the IR and media relations officers understand each other's jobs and work together. The IR staffer should be informed of any news releases going out to the media so that analysts aren't told one story at a meeting while the press gets a different version. That just destroys a company's credibility.

* * * * *

Beatrice Garcia is one of the nation's most recognized financial journalists. Her writing appears regularly in "Abreast of the Market" and "Heard on the Street" columns of *The Wall Street Journal*.

CREATING EFFECTIVE RELATIONSHIPS WITH EMPLOYEE-SHAREHOLDERS

Robert P. Greer
Sears, Roebuck and Company

One can make a strong case for the idea that stocks are *sold* rather than *bought*.

By this I mean to suggest that investor affairs, in its simplest terms, is necessarily a marketing function. Smart companies are marketing shares in much the same way as they would market products or services — through a carefully organized network of strategic communications.

Of course, even the most effective financial communications program has limits. Good communications will not substitute for quality performance and effective management. But all things being equal, the stock of a company that has maintained dialogue with the key segments of its investment universe is generally more highly valued than that of the one that has not done so.

It is the focus on segmenting the investment universe that I find essential here. Audience identification and priority assignments are vital to any marketing effort. This is particularly so with the discipline and practice of investor relations.

Fundamentally, there are two groups within the financial marketplace — those who *advise* and those who *invest*. They are equally important.

The advisors — broker and institutional analysts — often extract the lion's share of time and attention from the IR functions. This is understandable, given the sizable increase of institutional investors in the marketplace — an increase from 30 percent in 1980 to over 70 percent today. Although the institutional side dominates the majority of IR programs, I believe we must never lose sight of the individual shareholder.

To many IR practitioners, the "individual" is understood as the "active investor," whom I define as someone who trades 10 or more times annually. But, let us not forget that "other" individual shareholder — the employee-shareholder. It has long seemed to me that there are both special opportunities and problems associated with employee-shareholders, and therefore this group should be considered a unique marketing target.

POTENTIAL OPPORTUNITIES

On average, employees have a naturally receptive attitude toward the company, which grows more positive the longer an employee remains with the firm. Employees tend to feel as though few people can understand "their" company as well as those who make it work everyday.

Similarly, most employees appreciate having a sense of ownership in their company, however small or great. Such ownership proves to be a form of psychological equalization for employees. Stock ownership says, "We're all in this together," whether you labor in the mail room or the board room.

Another opportunity (and benefit) related to employee-shareholders is the vested interest they develop in their company's performance and stock valuation.

Yet another opportunity is afforded by the employee-shareholder base, which serves as a "captive audience." Since many company stock plans are tied to various forms of savings and pension programs, the employee-shareholder represents a steady and predictable level of stock acquisition.

POTENTIAL PROBLEMS

Perhaps the most common misunderstanding of this category of shareholders stems from the idea that all employee-shareholders are created equal. They are not. Not only do they vary widely in the corporate pecking order, they also have varied saving objectives and ambitions.

Employees also represent a broad spectrum of investment sophistication. Some may have a basic appreciation of the core workings of the equity market, while others know or care little. But few employee-shareholders, it can be presumed, have a deep understanding of the stock market and their particular company's participation in it. As a result, communications to the employee segment of the investor mix would do well to take an educational slant, as I will discuss later.

A CRITICAL AUDIENCE

Employee-shareholders are arguably a corporation's most vital audience. It should be obvious that in many companies employee-shareholders are a significant portion of total ownership as a consequence of employee investment plans, retirement programs, stock options, key management incentives, and dividend reinvestment.

It should be equally clear that it's the employee-shareholder who provides the company's creativity, productivity, and profitability, which drive stock price. Thus, employee morale and confidence become factors in the IR effort. Certainly a company with unfocused unrest in its employee ranks is a prime candidate for stock price erosion.

Further, employee-shareholders more often than not represent important allies and critical votes in the event of a takeover threat.

ESTABLISHING A BASE FOR EFFECTIVE COMMUNICATION

Given the significance and potential influence of the employee-shareholder, one should be careful to establish a solid base for effective communications with this special audience.

Too often companies make the mistake of treating employees like any other shareholder, assuming that all shareholder audiences will respond equally to the same communications.

Your first step should be to analyze the employee-shareholder make-up for your firm.

- What's the level or range of investor sophistication?
- What's the employee image of the company? How does that image compare with management's understanding of the company?
- What are the investment goals of the majority of your shareholders?
- Are there any burning corporate issues that concern employees?

Data for such baseline queries can often be obtained from periodic employee surveys. Such surveys not only provide core data useful to the design of an IR program, but they indicate to employees a level of active interest in employee opinion on the part of management.

DESIGNING EFFECTIVE COMMUNICATIONS

Once employee opinion has been surveyed and analyzed, the IR program needs to *set program objectives* and *develop communications strategies*.

In the area of *objectives*, decide what it is you want to accomplish with the employee-shareholder base — Consistent and predictable volume? Loyalty? Goodwill ambassadors? On-job performance and productivity? The chance to raise capital? The ability to defend against raiders?

Objectives should also take into consideration a timeframe. How much? How soon? How long?

Also consider available resources. Don't create too elaborate or ambitious a communications plan with employee-shareholders if you have a one-person IR function. On the other hand, if staff and related department assistance are available, aim for greater frequency of contacts and communication. The main point to remember here is to do a few things well and don't overextend or overpromise.

DEVELOPING THE STRATEGIES

Program strategy development should take into account at least six guideline considerations, especially as they relate to the employee perspective:

- Establish consistency of message.
- Make the message concise, clear, timely — you *are dealing with Main Street, not Wall Street.*
- Whatever you tell Wall Street, make sure Main Street hears about it in a timely and comprehensive fashion.
- Always aim to build credibility for the company, for management.
- Aim for a level of frequency — once a quarter, twice a quarter, more?
- Aim for a variety of communications vehicles and forums.

COMMUNICATING WITH EMPLOYEE-SHAREHOLDERS

Too often it seems IR programs target only the sophisticated audience of its analytical and institutional followings when it comes to both oral and written communications. Employees, it could be reasoned, are just along for the ride and therefore — intentionally or not — kept in the financial dark. This type of programming is not only unbalanced and short-sighted, it is potentially dangerous, especially in this era of the takeover.

The following key communications techniques have special application for employee-shareholders.

Oral Communication

1. *Annual Meeting.* Should have a component addressing employee contribution, special achievement, and hot issues.

2. *Meetings with Retirees.* Don't forget that retirees are part of the employee-shareholder mix. Some companies have been successful holding special receptions in conjunction with the annual meeting or other special events. This provides former employees a chance to interface with current management, which is often beneficial to both groups.

3. *Regional Employee Meetings.* Consider having the director of investor relations hold a series of employee meetings to clarify the value of the stock and purpose of the stock program, as well as provide a "state of the company" report.

4. *Telephone Inquiry Lines.* Some firms have established phone inquiry programs to answer employee questions.

5. *Brokers / Financial Planners.* Some firms make financial advisors available to assist employees in their overall estate and retirement planning.

Written Communications

1. *The Annual Report.* Look for opportunities to include the employee factor in the company's annual story.

2. *Quarterly Report.* The quarterly report extends opportunity to convey key employee messages.

3. *Welcome Shareholders Kit.* A regular flow of new employees could give rise to development of a Welcome Shareholder kit that describes the firm, the stock, and the plan and contains an employee survey card. Such a survey can serve as resource for ongoing input on employee-shareholder wants and needs.

4. *Employee Newsletters.* Most companies have newsletters. These are usually good vehicles in which to include news of the stock and stock-sensitive reports about the company.

5. *Letters from Management.* Consider issuing periodic letters from executive management on matters of general interest relative to the employee's investment, for instance, dividend announcements and reinvestment opportunities. It's also important to establish a quick system to communicate with employees in the event of special situations, such as takeover attempts, mergers and acquisitions, and stock repurchases. Sometimes a well-used system of interoffice memos can prove invaluable.

CONCLUSION

Don't overlook the influence and impact of employee-shareholders. And certainly don't take them for granted or keep them in the financial dark.

Work *for* and *with* them. Nurture their positive and proud appreciation of the company.

Above all, let them know they have a special stake in their own work and their own futures.

* * * * *

Robert P. Greer is assistant treasurer and director of corporate investor services for Sears, Roebuck and Company. Within the investors relations industry he is known as a leading practitioner of employee investor relations.

INTERNATIONAL INVESTOR RELATIONS

Alan Bulmer
City and Commercial Communications

'We now get invitations to lunch from at least four or five U.S. companies a day but never seem to hear much from them for the rest of the year.' — A leading U.K. Investment Director.

Most U.S. corporations have long since developed highly effective systems for communicating with their key institutional shareholders around North America. Unfortunately, far too many regard the international institutional arena as a minor item in their IR programme. As a consequence, they have come to rely on the once-a-year European road show, taking in the major financial centres — London, Geneva, Paris, and Frankfurt — with the occasional minor centre thrown in. The assumption is that, given an invitation, those institutions interested in the stock will attend. I believe that such traditional methods are no longer suitable for the fast-changing structure of international securities trading and fund management.

THE ROLE FOR EUROPE

Europe is no stranger to the financing of U.S. corporate growth; in the last century, for instance, many of the U.S. railroads were financed by British and European investors.

In this century, many U.S. corporations have already turned to these overseas financial markets as an important source of capital from outside their domestic base. The Eurobond market is now seen as a key and very sizeable alternative for U.S. and Canadian bond issuers, and, although the raising of equity capital overseas has proceeded at a rather slower pace, the current spate of new issues and secondary financing is such that the Euro-equity market should now be regarded as a key opportunity.

Recent years have seen many U.S. corporations listing their stock on European exchanges. Not only does this help to increase the investment following, but it also provides a useful base, for instance, for overseas securities issues.

Furthermore, the growing impact of 24-hour securities markets means that a listing on local exchanges may well prove to be a key factor in establishing wider trading of a corporation's stock around the world.

Most European exchanges have responded to the need for longer trading hours by installing new systems for electronic quotation and trading; at the same time, they have liberalised many of the rules that in the past prohibited local trading of overseas stocks.

THE KEY EUROPEAN CENTRES

The traditional pattern for investor presentations around Europe has tended to focus on five key centres — London, Zurich, Geneva, Paris, and Frankfurt — and these are still the most significant in terms of funds under management, with London holding a clear lead. The dominance of London becomes even more marked when allowance is made for its growing importance in the global, 24-hour securities market.

There are already signs that many European institutions are concentrating fund management in London in order to take advantage of the first-class trading facilities as well as of the greater availability of information and research capability.

This trend is particularly evident from the growing number of Japanese institutions that have chosen to base their international fund management operations in London. It has been matched by an increasing number of London-based fund management groups opening offices in New York and Tokyo, so that not only can portfolios be managed internationally but advantage can also be taken of the ability to trade on any significant developments at any time within the 24-hour day.

LONDON AFTER THE "BIG BANG"

Deregulation of the stockbroking community in London resulted not only in a large number of mergers within the U.K. fraternity, but also in a remarkable volume of purchases of U.K. stockbroking companies by banks and institutions from all parts of Europe and the Far East. Owners of London stockbroking companies now range from the Swiss Bank to the Hong Kong and Shanghai Bank, as well as major U.S. stockbroking names such as Shearson Lehman — where the decision was to acquire existing London companies rather than develop their own international capability.

The problem for the U.S. corporation in choosing which financial centre to visit on any specific trip is that the time constraints on senior management often limit the opportunity to extend IR coverage to the smaller centres. This is not so much of a problem when the U.S. corporation has several overseas subsidiaries, so that management can combine visits to these local operations with a presentation to the investment community.

Such a presentation can often be arranged at relatively short notice by an IR professional located in Europe, who will have an accurate and very detailed knowledge of the right institutions and individuals. It's simply a matter of specifying which of some 1500 names and institutions around Europe have a particular interest in the company in question.

WHO IS THE OVERSEAS SHAREHOLDER?

Perhaps the diffidence of so many U.S. corporations towards the international investment arena can be explained by the fact that accurate information on the size — and location — of overseas holdings is far from easy to obtain. In part, this is because so many overseas institutions disguise their presence behind marking names and other subterfuges. But it is also a result of the many changes in fund management business since the Big Bang which make it difficult to discover just who is actually managing a particular portfolio shown as a holder in your existing records.

Despite these difficulties, it is essential for a U.S. corporation to determine the current level of overseas shareholdings and to assess the percentage it would like to see held overseas in the future.

MORE THAN MEETS THE EYE

No company should underestimate the volume of overseas shareholders. Our own investigations on behalf of client corporations have shown that, behind various marking names and such, there lurks a far higher percentage of overseas shareholders than had been supposed. In one recent case, a survey for a major Fortune 500 company of published information by mutual funds and closed-end funds in London showed a figure for shares owned that was only 15 percent of the actual holdings of seven leading merchant banks.

Further detailed surveys revealed substantial holdings by insurance companies and pension funds, so that the final figure for London alone was well above 10 percent of the shares outstanding. As a result, the company needed to revise dramatically its international IR programme.

One medium-size U.S. corporation, admittedly with an excellent record but which developed an effective and long-term programme, has seen the percentage of overseas shareholders growing steadily from around 15 percent some five years ago to the present level of 36 percent of all shares outstanding. Even this figure may, in fact, be too low, since a number of holdings remain untraceable.

The bulk of the holdings not readily apparent to a company are those held by pension funds, investment trusts and discretionary funds for clients of merchant banks. It is interesting to note, too, that 80 percent of the shares in major U.K.-quoted companies are held on nominee accounts. Now, although most are held in nominee names for convenience rather than for any particular subterfuge, the nominee accounts do pose a considerable problem for those seeking to establish actual share ownership.

THE OVERSEAS SHAREHOLDER'S COMMITMENT

International shareholders have become increasingly aware that they can be an important influence on the company. Many have, for instance, taken quite strong and public stands on the appropriateness of antitakeover measures introduced by companies to safeguard existing management. Others have been very reluctant to exercise proxies and, although this response is now tending to change, it is important that institutions should know the best means of finding accurate information as to how their proxies should be exercised. Where existing management has made little effort to inform its overseas shareholders, it should not be surprised to find them supporting a takeover bid.

PERFORMANCE INVESTING

Behind the multitude of unknown holdings, of course, lurks an increasingly varied attitude towards investment performance. No longer should Europe be regarded as solely interested in stable long-term performance.

The cult of performance management is well-established throughout the major financial centres, and fund managers are tending to trim from their portfolios those companies about which they have only limited information on day-to-day business prospects. For the remaining holdings, fund managers require a good understanding of long-term capability, and they are quick to act on information that is relevant to a company's share price, as is evident from the growing volume of trading in U.S. stock that takes place outside the trading hours of the NYSE.

While such brokers as Jeffries and Company have long been active in trading large volumes of shares among European investors, there is now an active morning market in U.S. stocks in London, with market-makers from the major U.S. brokerage houses, such as Salomon, Morgan Stanley, and Goldman Sachs.

Nevertheless, international fund managers can be very supportive of the U.S. company through earnings difficulties — provided that they are kept fully informed. The need to meet performance targets may well result in a reduction in the amount of stock held, but often a small holding, or at the very least an active interest in the affairs of the company, is maintained.

A well-established, direct link with the IR officers and management of the company can be particularly effective at those moments when the institutional fund manager feels disadvantaged by poor research coverage or by a wrong assessment of the company's outlook by a broker's analyst.

GETTING TO KNOW THEM

Now, I have said a lot about the difficulties of obtaining the essential information on the whereabouts of shareholders and have suggested that some of the traditional methods of communicating with them may be open to question. So, it is time I offered a new approach to the task.

I believe that the most efficient way to identify shareholdings around Europe is to establish a close relationship with — and knowledge of — the fund management community in each overseas centre. It is a fact, for instance, that many fund management groups are quite happy to disclose the level of their holdings, provided such information is not allowed to reach the brokerage community at large but is restricted to the company's own use.

Unfortunately, the demands being placed on a fund manager's time are such that it is often difficult to obtain the relevant information. With global market-making enabling them to trade U.S. stocks from 7:00 A.M. London time right through to 9:00 P.M., with a growing number of United States brokers based in Europe and actively seeking to persuade the institutions to follow their particular research ideas, and with the great advances in electronic mail, desk-top publishing, and other forms of communication such as First Call, fund managers receive a volume of information that is far beyond what can be assimilated in the time available.

The only way to make really effective use of such limited time is to develop a close relationship with the key fund managers. In the new international investment environment, they are increasingly appreciative of a direct link into the company itself, preferring not to have to depend entirely for information on a research analyst or stockbroker. Not only is the speed of information flow critical to the maximising of investment performance, but the increased professionalism of the corporate IR manager also means that the fund manager can obtain a very accurate assessment of a company's prospects.

THE NEED TO SELECT

With so much detailed information available today on a wide variety of companies, a fund manager can effectively develop a true understanding of only a comparatively small group of key companies. In fact, many fund managers tend to follow a screened group of about 150 U.S. corporations that meet their main investment parameters and stretch across all sections of the economy, although they may at any one time be invested in only some 40 or 50 of them.

Most of us are constantly surprised by the wide variety of companies that appeal to international investors. With the growing diversity of individual mutual funds (perhaps specialising in recovery situations, small growth companies, energy, or even basic industry), there can often be a good response from investors, provided that the company in question has either good sustained earnings growth or the potential for a fast recovery from problems.

Where they have not been exposed to a company's product, investors are very responsive to management quality, especially if the company is, for instance, a small retailer or franchise. Most institutions do, in fact, state that it is not necessary for a company to visit Europe for its stock to be included in a portfolio, provided the right parameters are present. Even so, it certainly does help to get onto the list of 100 to 150 companies that are closely followed by any one institution.

It is also particularly vital for a corporation developing an international IR programme to ensure that it is included in that relatively small number of companies of which the fund manager has mental awareness when browsing through that foot-deep pile of daily research material. I have to admit that during my years as a fund manager in London I very rarely had the opportunity to develop in-depth research on any specific industry or company.

It is important to appreciate that very few international institutions have their own research teams, and indeed an "analyst" by name is often a junior fund manager in practice. Consequently, knowing where to obtain accurate and current information, from either a broker or some other source in North America, is particularly important for investor performance.

Indeed, now that great emphasis is placed on market-making and block trading, even overseas stockbroker sometimes find it difficult to develop fully an interesting investment idea with the depth of knowledge and understanding from his analyst that he would wish.

When you also take account of the different languages, cultures, and attitudes that apply in each financial centre in Europe and the Far East, it becomes even more clear just how difficult it is for the U.S.-based IR professional to develop a fully effective programme without assistance from specialised IR expertise located in the key financial centres.

BROKER-SPONSORED MEETINGS

One of the best sources of early information for the small U.S. corporation is the analysis of the European road show undertaken at the time the company becomes public. The broker involved with the issue will be able to provide full details on overseas shareholders at the time of issue, but it is thereafter that problems start to develop.

In the early stages of a company's development, the sponsoring broker fulfills a number of important roles and is often best-placed to assist with the initial IR programme in Europe. But when a company begins to receive analyst coverage from a number of U.S. or even international stockbrokers, then it is time for a more developed programme to be initiated.

Far too many U.S. corporations rely on a U.S. stockbroker to host a series of presentations around Europe and, although this has many attractions as a low-cost programme, it fails to reach the full audience. There is also very little "after-sales service," especially if the company's stock is only rated a hold or at worst a sell by the stockbroker concerned.

It is important for a corporation to visit all the stockbrokers who cover the company and who have offices in a particular financial centre — but this is hardly likely to happen if one stockbroker is hosting the visit.

Many sophisticated institutions around Europe now prefer to see a company's representative without any stockbroker present. The growing importance of trading, market-making, and position-taking by the major stockbroking houses is such that institutions are often reluctant to give any indication of their true attitude towards a particular company — and certainly tend not to ask their most detailed questions — when a broker is present.

The size of funds under management by the leading international management groups is such that many of the key institutions in Europe and the Far East merit a one-on-one visit by a corporation rather than an invitation to attend a large presentation.

Matters are further complicated by the likelihood of there being competition from four or five other corporations that have chosen to make a presentation in that particular financial centre on that particular day. Such is the popularity of road shows as a method of communication that it is by no means unusual for a fund manager to receive not only invitations from those four or five companies, but also to be offered presentations by analysts and seminars by trade associations. At the same time, the analyst is expected to devote some of the day to helping to market funds under management!

What this means, of course, is that many of the institutions represented in your stock may not be available to meet with your corporation during the visit. Yet again, this underlines the importance ensuring that an IR programme is not limited to the once-a-year road show approach to the international arena.

Since one cannot be all things to all people — and since the schedule for a visit to Europe may permit only a limited number of one-on-one meetings — it is most important to identify accurately those investment institutions that have a large representation in your stock.

THE IMPORTANCE OF THE REGIONAL BROKER

One factor that is not always readily appreciated by U.S. corporations is the major importance of the U.S. regional broker for overseas investors and their advisors. Many fund managers and analysts covering the United States are generalists by necessity, since they have little time to specialise in any particular industry. When the level of overseas investment was far smaller, the regional brokers found that local institutions in Europe's financial centres tended to be profitable to them, but less so to the major New York houses.

Furthermore, many regional or smaller U.S. brokers are able to provide in-depth research on a number of local companies, and this appealed to European investors who felt that they were not competing directly with the big guns of the major financial institutions. Leading international financial institutions still have a high regard for the level of opinion and advice that they receive from brokerage houses outside New York and still maintain a relatively high commission flow in return for these ideas.

Many of the institutional salespeople at these regional houses who talk to overseas institutions are perceived more as analysts than direct salespeople. Overseas fund managers have long been significant investors in emerging growth companies for similar reasons. In the early stages of the technology boom in San Francisco, for instance, many of the leading participants had a significant percentage of overseas shareholders, a factor that was in many ways attributable to the capabilities of the regional stockbrokers in San Francisco, who had long cultivated such overseas institutions.

Now that funds under management in overseas financial centres have grown to such a major size, there is of necessity a greater level of investment in top Fortune 500–type companies and demand for effective overseas IR programmes to match this interest. Having been for a time the fund manager of one of the largest U.S. portfolios in the world, though not located in the U.S., and having been for seven years an institutional salesman with two leading firms of U.S. stockbrokers, I can vouch for the fact that the level of overseas shareholdings in U.S. corporations is far higher than most such companies are aware.

DEVELOPING THE INTERNATIONAL PROGRAMME

Now, it will have become clear that I am arguing against the traditional broker-hosted "catch all" visit as the totality of a corporation's attempt at international IR activity. It has a place — but no more than that. It should be viewed as part of a planned, comprehensive programme.

Not that I am arguing, of course, for the idea of limiting the road show to those years in which results are good. The international fund manager is looking for continuity of information, even when the figures are not particularly impressive. A company that takes the trouble to explain its bad years as well as its good ones will gain credibility with the fund manager. Those who chose to cancel their trip to Europe at the time of the Libyan terrorist threat or who pleaded diplomatic illness when earnings results were not as good as forecast ran the risk of losing the attention and interest of the international investment community.

The key element in establishing an international IR programme is — as I have already intimated — determining the existing shareholder base. Only then can you formulate an effective plan to expand that shareholder base while at the same time increasing the information flow and level of understanding to the broad spectrum of international fund managers.

Normally this entails a detailed survey, by telephone and personal visit, of key institutions in each financial centre. Such a survey provides a useful starting point, but unless it is combined with a detailed assessment of institutional attitudes towards the particular company, the information may have only limited value. In many cases I have found that an institution's assessment of the company has very little in common with the company's own understanding of its particular strength and capability.

Far too many companies decide that it would be "a good thing" to go to Europe, especially perhaps to raise further capital or list on an exchange. But unless a detailed assessment is made of all areas of the company's visibility to institutions, an IR programme is in danger of reinforcing mistaken beliefs in the eyes of institutional investors. By "detailed assessment" I mean not only the capability of the IR department, but institutional attitudes towards senior management quality, trading practices, capabilities of individual subsidiaries, policies on mergers and acquisition, relative share price performance, availability of information, corporate communications capability, and a whole string of other factors.

Once the initial groundwork in establishing a company's level of shareholding and interest in Europe has been established, a programme combining many of the elements discussed above can be implemented. As I mentioned earlier, the road show should be only one of a number of coordinated strategies. Should you list on a variety of European exchanges? Should you appear at a number of conferences, trade shows, and presentations at local facilities or subsidiaries? These are only a few of the questions that need to be considered and that can contribute towards establishing a greater understanding of a company's capabilities.

The older, established conferences in Europe have proved a useful starting point for corporations unfamiliar with international investment attitudes and practices, but they also provide a rather expensive and inefficient introduction to the international community. Most companies soon resolve their own detailed programme, which does not conflict with the similar needs of a large number of other companies that may also be attending that conference. Many fund managers deliberately avoid such large conferences, since they feel that little relevant new information is likely to be released in front of such a broad and in some cases not particularly well-informed audience.

Far greater results tend to emerge from a programme that combines a series of one-on-one meetings, small lunch-time presentations, and analyst briefings. While most fund managers appreciate a good meal with an agreeable wine, this no longer forms a major part of their working day. The pressures of modern fund management are such that not only has the time available for presentations over lunch decreased, but many fund managers rarely even take any alcohol during the day.

The traditional invitation to a presentation at noon followed by lunch and finishing up at 2:30 P.M. is liable to receive a re-sounding "No" from the key fund managers to which a company should appeal and result in attendance by what can best be termed as "rent-a-crowd," provided by the corporate sponsor to ensure that the chairman has a sea of faces before him.

Far more can be achieved by inviting a select group of be-tween 10 and 20 fund managers who have a good understanding of the company or a particular interest in the industry to a hard-working lunch where the choice of food makes a positive rather than negative impression on an increasingly diet-conscious community.

The breakfast meeting is now a regular part of London investment life and has even become a growing factor in conti-nental Europe. It may be some years before this form of pre-sentation meets with any approval in Paris, but many fund managers in London find it a particularly efficient means of maximising their available time.

PRESENTATION TO AN INTERNATIONAL AUDIENCE

It is surprising how many U.S. corporate management teams still talk down to the audience as though it was totally unfamil-iar with the company. Far too often much of the presentation is taken up with reiterating the annual report, whereas most fund managers will already have done a good deal of initial research, even if they are unfamiliar with the company. It is much more productive to focus on future plans and leave plenty of time for an extensive question-and-answer period in which key strategies can be brought out.

Fund managers in Europe are exposed to so many companies, with as many as four or five a day presenting London alone, that it is important to build in a key theme, linking the various strategies, that can be implanted in the fund manager's mind as a clear, simple identification of a company's approach. Once a key theme has been developed, it can then be enhanced by reiteration through a corporate communications programme, which might include, for instance, a series of financial advertisements placed to coincide with publication of the company's results in order to enhance investor awareness.

POST-MEETING ANALYSIS

The effective postmeeting and premeeting analysis of institutional opinion and shareholdings is a vital but often overlooked constituent of effective investor relations in Europe. It is particularly difficult to monitor trading activity by international institutions even with the close cooperation of the company itself in the United States. Few exchanges and few of the growing number of international market-makers provide any detailed reporting on volume figures, and a higher degree of trust needs to be established with fund managers and brokers for such information to be disclosed.

It is important that the Europe-based IR professional is seen as an extension of the company, so that fund managers do not feel that their information on stockholding will be disclosed to a wider audience. There is a growing resistance to providing information, not least as a result of the mass of telephone surveys conducted by public relations organisations. The telephone defences of the more experienced institutional fund managers are constructed not only to keep the unwelcome broker at bay, but also to minimise time-wasting calls from a number of directions. Surveys by letter offer some benefit in terms of providing detailed addition to the database, but unfortunately the response rate is low.

Only by knowing who are the key individuals in each institution and being able to reach them with pertinent information is it possible to establish a truly beneficial interchange of information. Not only are fund managers reducing the number of brokers with whom they deal, they are also cutting back on the number of companies followed. One major merchant bank in the United Kingdom has now limited its U.S. holdings to between 30 and 40 individual companies at any one time. This makes it very difficult to get across to the institution that a fundamental change has taken place in a particular company and that they can once again reinstate an investment position.

When monitoring the response to corporate presentations after the event, it is rare to find an immediate surge of buying or selling interest on the part of institutions unless some particularly important change has been announced. However, these presentations often instigate a reassessment of a holding or plant the seeds for the initiation of a buying programme. Even so, market timing remains the critical factor, and it will often be the release of a brokerage recommendation or some other event that finally sparks the change in a holding. Indeed, it is interesting to note that new research reports on companies now have more impact when they are first mentioned at a brokers' morning meeting than when the report is finally issued. Such is the thirst for more and more immediate information.

RETAIL INVESTORS

Retail investors are as yet too few in number to have any immediate importance, but the growing private client presence by the major U.S. stockbrokers and increased emphasis by domestic brokers are an indication of a future need. The reply coupon at the foot of selective corporate financial advertising is already bringing in a growing number of responses from individuals. At present, the broad range of individual investors is well-catered to by the huge number of mutual funds. There are approximately 1,000 different individual funds in the United Kingdom alone.

Deregulation and privatisation around Europe have created millions of new shareholders, and with the boom conditions of most stockmarkets, greater personal affluence means that it is just a matter of time before the individual shareholder becomes sufficiently important to be the target of planned IR coverage. Perhaps one of the first steps might be the teleconferencing of annual meetings to London and Tokyo as well as to key centres in the United States.

INSTITUTIONAL INVESTOR VISITS TO THE UNITED STATES

For many years a number of European institutional investors have regularly visited corporate facilities in the United States during their various fact-finding tours. There is also a growing number of group tours organised by either international or U.S. stockbrokers.

One example is the 70-strong group of U.K. analysts and fund managers taken to North America on the Concorde by a leading drinks company at a cost of some £500,000.

International investors are always keen to know well in advance about any special presentations organised at a company's U.S. facilities so they can include a visit in their next fact-finding tour. At the same time the European-based IR practitioner should be a regular visitor at the various key facilities of any corporate client in the United States.

LISTING ON INTERNATIONAL EXCHANGES — IS IT WORTH IT?

The complexity of listing regulations on European stock exchanges, especially London, is such that all listings of U.S. companies are becoming a costly exercise. Whereas in the past it was possible to arrange a listing within a budget of, say $60,000, there is now likely to be no change from $300,000 owing to the necessity for a wide number of accountants, lawyers, brokers, and bankers to be involved.

Nevertheless, the listing of a company's shares on the London Exchange, for instance, is becoming perhaps more of an important step and less of a publicity exercise than had hitherto been the case. The growth of a global, 24-hour marketplace in the shares of leading corporations means that the local exchange will often insist that the company's shares be listed on that exchange in order for trading to take place outside the hours of the New York market. Even so, the high cost of arranging this listing is such that it is vital to obtain the maximum benefit by integrating the listing with a comprehensive communications and IR campaign.

The U.S. company listed in London is competing not only with some 220 other U.S. companies out of the 2,700 companies listed, but with a whole host of Japanese, European, and Scandinavian companies. The U.S. companies account for only 40 percent of all foreign companies listed in London, and although no accurate figures have ever been obtained for the volume of foreign share trading on the London Exchange, it has been estimated that this accounts for some 10 percent of overall trading volume.

Perhaps the key benefit to a corporation's listing on European exchanges is that access to local capital markets is enhanced. While it is not absolutely essential to be listed on any local exchange, many companies have found that not having an established presence in those markets can considerably raise the cost of any financing undertaken. Similarly, an extensive programme of IR that has increased the demand for the company's shares and created a widespread pool of shareholders considerably facilitates the raising of either equity or bond finance at a later date.

A broad shareholder base spread throughout the international financial markets enhances stability at a time when the greater efficiency of the world marketplace in evaluating information can increase volatility. Nevertheless, there are widely varying national characteristics that apply just as much to investors, and it is not unusual for totally different opinions on a company to exist in, say, Zurich and London. Furthermore, major currency swings have made it almost more important to be right on the local currency relationship with the dollar than with the underlying trend of Wall Street.

There are still some countries where local regulations restrict the purchase of nonlisted shares, for instance by insurance companies in France, but by large these regulations are being dismantled and local stockmarkets opened up to overseas competition.

The growing number of international mergers has had a particular impact on overseas listing and shareholder relations. An efficient programme can produce a large spread of loyal shareholders who are likely to support the company in such a situation. The reverse can also be true where little effort has been made on part of the company.

It is indeed surprising how many U.S. corporations with a high proportion of overseas earnings and sales pay little attention to establishing a relatively high proportion of overseas shareholders. These corporations often have a considerable advantage in embarking on such a programme, not least by reason of the familiarity of the overseas shareholder with the company's products and presence in that country. Such corporations as IBM, Pepsi Cola, Coca Cola, and General Motors are household words in every corner of the world, and indeed IBM for many years has held a series of international shareholder presentations at its factories around the world.

A COORDINATED PROGRAMME OF CORPORATE COMMUNICATIONS

The growing sophistication of the international fund manage ment arena is such that a well coordinated corporate communications programme is essential. Fund managers are burdened with so much information — electronic, printed, or by telephone — that they have only a limited ability to assimilate key factors and also to sift through this vast area of information.

By combining an IR programme with the use of other media, the corporation can transform its profile and capabilities. A tactical financial advertising campaign can raise the company's profile in Europe by maintaining the awareness of its achievements and by increasing the understanding of its corporate strategy.

One instance of such a strategy might well be the use of limited financial advertising in key national newspapers during the period when a company is making presentations in Europe to the various financial communities. This does not need to be a massive advertising campaign (which, quite frankly, can often be counterproductive in the fund manager's eyes), but instead a series of limited campaigns focusing on the vitality of the company or perhaps repositioning its corporate strategy.

While advertising provides a unique degree of control and consistency in delivering the corporate message, it can be further enhanced by a flexible and cost-effective press relations programme. Editorial coverage is relatively easy to obtain in some countries, but rather more difficult in a key financial centre such as London. The *Financial Times* and *The Wall Street Journal Europe* are probably the most effective means of communicating to the European financial community as a whole.

While a press conference during a European visit is a good way of disseminating information, it should be used only when there is particularly interesting or "hard" news to convey to the community. I usually prefer to recommend one-on-one press meetings, which enable a journalist to obtain more detailed and varied information.

Consequently such meetings tend to attract the more knowledgeable and senior journalists, and this enhances the likelihood of positive, well-informed and factually correct press coverage. Financial institutions are most reluctant to see journalists included in normal corporate presentations, and so press meetings should be a separate part of the programme. Nevertheless, a hard copy of the presentations and speeches will be well-received by journalists, especially if a synopsis of the key questions and answers is also included.

The corporate communications programme can be further complemented by an effective means of transmitting the company's interim and final results together with other key announcements to the media throughout Europe. There are now many systems — ranging from electronic mail and facsimile to the traditional hand delivery of press releases — that can ensure that a company's results reach the European communities at the same time as they are released in New York.

This does pose some problems in terms of the timing of the release of corporate information, especially since global trading of a company's shares may well mean that there are open and active markets in Europe in the stock while New York and Tokyo are still asleep. As there is no particular remedy to this problem, however, I suggest that timing should be arranged to coincide with the greatest market availability — in other words, when New York is open and fund managers around the rest of the world will be following the progress of the New York market on their various electronic media.

KEEPING THE INFORMATION FLOWING

In addition to the various corporate communications outlined above, a comprehensive mailing service allows the specific targetting of key fund managers, analysts, and brokers for annual reports, interim results, and other releases. While a number of databases are available for the dissemination of material, relatively few are designed specifically for targetting key individuals responsive to that information rather than blanket coverage to all listed names. Most general information will be readily dispatched to the institution's library, yet detailed and timely information, such as an analyst presentation in New York, can be a very positive contribution if received by international fund managers before it is out of date.

Additional information that should be provided to international shareholders on a regular basis includes major research reports or new coverage by analysts starting to follow the company and accounts of any important developments covered in the U.S. but perhaps not by the international media, such as a key article in Business Week, Barons, or Fortune. A summary of major analyst presentations, in the form of speeches and full details on the question-and-answer period, together with any briefing summary sent out on a regular basis to the analyst community, are all well-received and could easily be combined into the format of a newsletter on a regular basis.

THE EXPANSION OF ANALYST COVERAGE ABROAD

The disadvantages of using one particular broker to arrange an international road show or series of presentations are further compounded by the growing extent of international research and analysis. This is now being undertaken not only by the fund management institutions, but, most important, by the newly created international brokerage concerns in London and the rest of Europe. It should also be noted that a number of the major Japanese brokerage houses have established research teams in the European centres, mainly in London.

A growing trend for analysts is to cover all major companies within their sector on an international rather than purely domestic basis. In other words, a chemical analyst based in London will now follow not only a leading U.K. name, such as ICI, but will also be actively involved in, say, Dupont, as well as the leading Japanese and Swiss companies. It is worthwhile arranging a special briefing session for analysts so that they can gain a detailed understanding of the workings of a U.S. company; this involves a rather different format of presentation than might have been undertaken for fund managers.

Most managers of the large international fund tend to be generalist in their approach rather than having the level of detailed and specific knowledge on one industry that an analyst might achieve. These analyst meetings can also be combined with a detailed briefing of some of the representatives of the U.S. stockbroking companies who have offices in that city; of course, this fulfils a second function in that fund managers and brokers are kept separate. Far too often an excellent research report by a U.S. analyst who is regarded highly for his or her knowledge of the company fails to have any influence overseas unless a particular institutional sales team has familiarized itself with the report.

New technology available to the IR professional is quickly transforming the international IR programme. It is now by no means unusual to plan a satellite conference linking a presentation to U.S. analysts and shareholders with groups of European shareholders in a number of key financial centres. This can be particularly effective in special circumstances, such as a major takeover or a new issue, and certainly helps to solve the problem of timing the release of important information to reach as wide an audience as possible.

INTERNATIONAL IR CONSULTANTS — WHAT CAN A LOCAL GROUP PROVIDE?

In assessing the need for an overseas-based IR capability and deciding how best to utilize such a facility in terms of the massive and constant change in the financial environment overseas, it is important to select a consultancy that has in-depth experience of both fund management and broking, so that it can provide fully comprehensive advice to the corporation.

Investor relations as a profession is less understood by the institutions in Europe, so individuals with a background in either fund management or broking have a greater ability to confer at senior level with fund managers and their directors. Inexperienced individuals will have great difficulty in obtaining the information that is released only by such institutions on a very discretionary basis.

Investor relations in Europe is, of necessity, becoming more and more specialised, yet there are relatively few providers of in-depth service and capability that are more than just the abilities of a travel agent to arrange road shows. The locally based IR consultant has to operate as a virtual office of the company if a fully comprehensive service is to be provided, and this can only be achieved for a carefully controlled number of companies.

Current trends in overseas IR include the ability to offer day-to-day communications with the corporate client and advise not only on institutional contact but also on the abilities of local analysts, the market-makers in the stock of the corporation on the local exchange, relationships with the financial press, and, of course, the effective dissemination of accurate information.

Historically, most Europe-based IR companies have been located in either Switzerland or Brussels, but the growing importance of London as a major financial centre necessitates an on-the-spot presence with skilled personnel. Within our own organisation, I feel that the best balance is fulfilled by a combination of the two, in other words, effective organisation on the ground in both London and Zurich, inasmuch as the many languages and variations of the individual continental European centres are more applicable to the Zurich than to the London office. This is also a reflection of the very large number of institutions and brokers based in London in terms of maximising the effective use of personnel. This chapter has tended to focus on the United Kingdom and continental Europe because the greater part of international funds under management are located in those areas.

Nevertheless, Japan is, of course, now the largest stock market in the world, but in terms of IR probably the least developed. As I mentioned earlier, a considerable proportion of Japanese investment management in overseas stocks has been located either in New York or in London, rather than domestically in Japan. Indeed, Japan is a difficult area for a non-Japanese IR professional, since the whole concept is as yet little understood there. Only five or so Japanese corporations employ in-house IR professionals and the number of specialised IR companies is relatively limited. In view of the particular constraints of the Japanese market and the deeply embedded resistance to any foreign interference, a U.S. corporation is perhaps better served by using one of the major Japanese brokers to coordinate any presentations made in that country.

SOME POINTS TO REMEMBER

Much of this chapter has focused on reasons why companies should consider an international IR programme; however, there are many times when a road show can be counterproductive and may lead to a negative attitude that can linger on for many years. It is not an infrequent event to hear a fund manager respond to an invitation with "Oh, I am not interested in that company, they let me down very badly some five (or even ten) years ago." The following list is not meant to be definitive, but merely an indication of some of the problem areas.

An international road show may not be beneficial

- If the firm is publicizing a new issue or financing where insufficient stock is available to the overseas investor.
- When a company is seen to be combining the trip too obviously with a vacation.
- Where the response is likely to be "I am not interested in that stock; they only come over when the earnings are good."
- Where a company has gone ex-growth or is just badly managed.
- Where an annual visit is too obviously sponsored by a broker as a corporate finance duty, yet where there is no research or sales effort devoted to that company during the rest of the year.
- Where a company only reviews the annual report and refuses to give any indication of the future and how they intend to manage it.
- Where the audience has been invited to a presentation for the sake of numbers rather than selectivity — the "rent-a-crowd" approach is often very obvious.
- During the high season of spring and autumn, where often there are conflicting meetings of equally attractive companies. The number of international fund managers in each financial centre is finite.
- Finally, in Paris in August, as this is still the time at which the majority of the city takes its annual vacation.

I have endeavoured to give a broad overview of some of the key aspects of international IR rather than dwelling in detail on the exact investment figures or the particular complexities of each individual financial centre. Many of these subjects are worthy of a chapter of their own, not least the merits of listing a company's shares on the various exchanges around the world. Let me say, in conclusion, that the aims of an effective international IR programme are to spread the knowledge, involvement, and understanding of a corporation throughout the various financial centres. If fully achieved, this will greatly facilitate raising money, by bond or by equity, in any currency or financial centre. Widespread awareness of the merits of a company allow it the option to choose not only the timing of a financing, but also the location and currency that best suit the company's interest.

* * * * *

Alan Bulmer is a principal of City and Commercial Communications, a noted international investor relations counsel in London with extensive dealings throughout Europe and the Far East.

INVESTOR RELATIONS FOR THE OVER-THE-COUNTER COMPANY

Donald Kirsch
The Wall Street Group

There are many justifiable reasons for inviting public participation in the growth of a corporation, but none so compelling as the creation of a corporate currency that can be used for acquisitions and financings with as little dilution to shareholders as is reasonable. For the securities of a public company to be transformed into a corporate currency, the shares must at all times maintain three pivotal ingredients: (1) a high, sustainable PE ratio relative to other companies in the industry category; (2) good geographic distribution; and (3) excellent marketability. All three hinge on the proper interweaving of support from shareholders, market-makers, stockbrokers, security analysts, and buy-side financial professionals such as money managers, portfolio advisors, and trust and estate officers.

Each of these represents a constituent audience with special requirements. The common denominator is that all need information with which to make investment decisions, and the tactical approach to creating an honest program to which they respond is the art of financial public relations. Strong underlying principles of good communication pertain to all financial public relations programs for all companies. However, the over-the-counter (OTC) market presents a terraced landscape that requires different techniques of cultivation for "pink sheet" stocks, supplementary listed securities, and those that are fortunate enough to be listed on the national market system. A separate approach is also dictated for the newly public enterprise, wherever it finds itself in the OTC trading mechanism.

One must remember that prices of all securities represent a temporary agreement between speculators; this is nowhere more evident than in the OTC universe, a dealer-oriented market much removed from and in many cases more desirable than an auction market. The appeal of a stock is as much in how it is perceived as in its reality, and marketing the image of an OTC stock blends the dissimilar disciplines of financial analysis and advertising. However, a program resting on hype and hope is doomed to failure; one anchored by demographic research and bolstered by market analysis has an opportunity to succeed.

Some 45,000 U.S. corporations have sufficient shareholders to be deemed publicly owned companies. Of these, approximately 18,000 trade actively, and the remainder so rarely that Wall Streeters refer to them as securities that are bought and sold "by appointment." Growth companies, by their very composition, have an incessant requirement for capital. True growth companies will always grow faster than their cash flow and bank lines, and inevitably must turn to the public marketplace to generate the equity and debt that will permit them to capitalize on the opportunities created by their unusual product or service.

In the race for investment capital, the winner is always the company with loyal and dedicated financial sponsorship. Given the premise that the interests of management and shareholders are consistent only as long as the company and its securities prosper, the public corporation not only must exhibit unusual growth, but must position its securities in a fashion that distinguishes them from other investment vehicles. Having had the opportunity over three decades of introducing the earliest public entries in numerous industries, such as mobile homes and cable television in the 60s, independent software companies in the 70s, and controlled-release technology and genetic pharmaceuticals in the 80s, we have found that the strongest and most successful financial sponsorship programs inevitably are supported by excellent demographic analysis.

As a result, we begin the blocking out of a new program with what we term KSPs — key selling propositions — which enable us in quick strokes to catch the attention of a potential financial sponsor. Alongside this, we outline the specific objectives we hope to attain over a 24-month horizon. In the case of the mobile home industry a quarter of a century ago, the KSPs were:

1. The annual growth of mobile homes as a percentage of nonfarm housing starts.
2. The cost of the dwelling per square foot as opposed to the cost of stick building.
3. The modest loss ratio of mobile home paper as compared with that of automobile paper.
4. The cost per mile of moving a mobile home and the average tenure of residency in a single location.
5. The percentage of PTA affiliation for families with school-aged children, and the percentage of church affiliation for all mobile home dwellers.

The purpose of this exercise was to quickly demonstrate that mobile home dwellers, although selecting an alternative life style, were stable and community conscious, and that cost factors had created a primary industry growth trend in which a number of good manufacturers could participate. Within this strong primary trend, we then deposited the numbers of the growth company we represented, Skyline Homes, Inc., a company that went on to become one of the great industrial success stories.

In the case of Health-Chem Corporation, a diversified corporation redeploying assets from stable but unexciting markets to support a growing involvement in controlled-release technology, the KSPs were:

1. The number of pharmaceutical products coming off patent whose life could be extended by encapsulation in a controlled-release format.
2. The medical benefits of a delivery system that permitted release over a prolonged period of time on a systemic basis or a specific area basis.
3. The size of market in agricultural applications, with demographics specific to each type of crop for which Health-Chem was developing a herbicidal or fungicidal delivery system.

Using a demographic approach to the industry group accents the primary trend available to all manufacturers in the group and gives the possible investor an opportunity to measure the potential of the specific company against that of the other players. In a new industry, with no one yet demonstrating earnings and with 129 patents of its own, Health-Chem Corporation quickly became a market favorite. In the first 18 months of the program, a review of broadly capitalized stocks by *The Economist* ranked Health-Chem Corporation first in the United States and second in the world in growth of market valuation over the preceding 12 months.

Of course, the expansion of a company's PE multiple, integral to its financing capabilities, rests on more than KSPs. Managements of public companies quite correctly focus a great deal of attention on the company's PE multiple, but less visible and equally important objectives should be part of the financial public relations program. The improvement in trading volume, or liquidity of investment, and the broad dispersion of shares solve certain problems unique to public companies.

For instance, the accumulation of shares by an institutional investor carries not only the delight of support but the possibility of share price destruction. An appropriate ingredient of a financial public relations program is the creation of sufficient trading involvement in the company's securities so that disposal of a large block of shares by an institution can be accommodated without wrecking the support barrier and injuring every shareholder. Equally important, in an economic climate that encourages corporate muggers who prefer to seize a company's assets rather than build their own, is the broad diversification of shareholders, both regionally among individual stock buyers and by different types of financial institutions. Shares held by financial institutions with long horizons are certainly more preferable than large shareholding interests by hedge funds, although hedge-fund operators bring a degree of liquidity to the marketplace.

Therefore, a broad dispersion of shares throughout several investment communities in the United States and abroad should be a goal equal to the goal of an expanded PE multiple. In this ambition, an effort should be made to balance individual holdings against institutional commitments. Again, these three elements — a sustainable high PE multiple (in relation to others in the industry group), broad geographic distribution, and marketability or liquidity — represent true sponsorship for your corporate currency. These are appropriate goals for the management of a public company, and are reasonable if the company indeed does have strong growth prospects. One must be realistic about one's own prospects: An underwear manufacturer will not sport the same PE multiple as a genetic engineering company, but in turn the acquisitions to be made by the underwear manufacturer can be accomplished at much lower prices than those in the gene-splicing business. If the underwear manufacturer's corporate currency carries a PE multiple higher than that of its public or private competitor, the manufacturer can use that fact just as successfully in its acquisition program.

A rational criterion for a successful financial public relations program is essential in the development of one's strategy. A company early on must decide whether it wishes to encourage speculation in its securities for the sake of an extra notch or two in its PE multiple, or seek out instead long-term support, which is not easily won and not easily lost.

Maneuvering between the desire for a sustainable, high PE ratio and the perils of support from speculators is more grueling for the managements of OTC companies than for firms listed on major exchanges. However, the creation of a national market system has brought a level of professionalism to much of the OTC market, along with work of a quality frequently difficult to match on most exchanges.

CREATING THE PROGRAM

The most important element in a financial sponsorship program is candor. Management should at all times be prepared to discuss anything allowed by SEC rules, and all subjects that will not reduce the company's competitive posture if other companies receive the information.

With KSPs defined and realistic goals developed (i.e., 24-month objectives for the PE multiple, the number and type of shareholders, and the trading volume), one must attend to the creation of collateral materials that will be useful in such a program. An up-to-date press kit should be available at all times for presentation not only to newspeople but to members of the financial community. The kit should include the most recent 10-K, any 10-Qs subsequent to the most recent 10-K, and any 8-Ks filed in the past year. One should also include a chronological file of press releases, from the most recent through those put out 12 months ago, trade as well as financial, plus copies of advertisements either recently run or scheduled to run in the near future. Reprints of articles about the company and trend analysis of the industry are also helpful. Independent market letters relating to the industry or the company specifically are always useful provided they are still timely, as are reprints of speeches before analyst societies. The most recent printed annual report for shareholders plus any subsequent quarterly reports should also be included.

The press kit should be kept up-to-date, with materials older than 12 months removed as new materials are added. It is wise to keep as many as two to three dozen kits available at all times so that one can quickly respond to inquiries, for instance, if broad interest should develop as a result of publicity or the attention of an advisory letter writer.

Two other collaterals are invaluable. The first, a corporate profile, should be limited to a single page, printed front and back, containing at the head such information as most recent sales, earnings, PE ratio, trailing 12 months, estimated forward 12 months, estimated PE ratio, capitalization, float, and market makers. Follow this information with a summary paragraph, avoiding purchase recommendations. It is important to remember that this is to be a report, not a market advisory statement. Follow the summary paragraph with an analysis, in greater detail, of the separate operations of the business, listing product lines, demographic figures, and competitors. An abbreviated balance sheet and a chart of the stock's action are also helpful.

The second invaluable collateral is a film or slide presentation — aimed at the financial community but also usable at annual meetings, this can be extremely helpful in telling the corporate story. Bear in mind that the formal portion of a presentation to brokers or analysts should not exceed 20 minutes, and that a slide presentation therefore should probably not include more than 30 to 40 slides, depending upon the cadence of the speaker.

With KSPs defined, objectives stated, and collaterals prepared, a 24-month program should be scheduled, with each of the 24 months divided into four program segments: financial community contact, publicity, shareholder reports, and special events.

Financial Community Contacts

There are in the United States and Canada today 53 societies of financial and securities analysts, comprising some 16,000 individual members, and numerous groups formed or in formation in Europe and parts of Asia. All these stem from the founding in 1937 of the New York Society of Security Analysts, an organization initially composed of statisticians who sharply upgraded their calling; they evolved into a body of professionals whose approval or rejection frequently decides the financing capability of a public corporation.

Analysts favor companies with high visibility. It makes it easier for them to write about the company if it is widely known and widely followed. Therefore, a policy of quarterly regional analysts' meetings is mandatory in a contemporary financial public relations program.

However, the meeting must be well-planned. A corporate press kit should be available with the latest information, as well as some historical data for those who are newcomers. Management should be prepared to speak for 20 minutes and then to answer questions. A formal invitation should follow a telephone invitation, and a reminder call should be made the morning of the meeting. Follow-up calls should be made to key individuals at the meeting to see if any questions were unsatisfactorily answered or if questions that should have been raised were overlooked. Before setting a meeting check with the local broker and analyst societies to see whether others speaking on that day will create a conflict for the audience you have in mind.

Annually, a meeting should be held before one of the constituent societies of the Financial Analyst Federation or a stockbroker society of size and reputation. A written speech should be available and reprinted and sent to shareholders, market makers, brokers, and other interested parties. Press should always be invited.

Most analyst societies require that a company not speak to any other financial analyst society for some period prior to appearing before that group. This usually does not apply to hand-picked invitational meetings, but you should check in advance. In preparing a 24-month speaking calendar, plan one speaking engagement each quarter and diversify the meetings not only geographically but among special interest groups. Many industries have splinter groups of security analysts who follow that specialty, and meetings before these organizations can be even more fruitful than those before one of the major analyst societies. Invitational meetings are most productive when they are small, two dozen or so, and should be specifically aimed at target audiences: brokers, analysts, money managers, or market-makers. Although one has to be flexible about these things, too frequently information of interest to one group is boring to another, and mixing the groups creates listless meetings.

In dealing with the professional financial community, OTC companies must distinguish between the needs of market-makers, stockbrokers, financial analysts, and money managers.

Market-makers are interested principally in activity in a company's stock. They should have a full kit of material on the company and its history and should be kept abreast of all new developments through press releases and telephone calls after the press releases have run on one of the newswires.

In seeking market-makers, turn first to those brokerage houses closest to your corporate headquarters. Visit individually with the market-maker after the close of trading, bringing with you the full background kit on the company and especially a brief corporate profile. A good annual report is very useful. The approach to the market-maker should be restricted to the chief executive officer, the chief operating officer, or the chief financial officer.

Market-makers are very responsive to their own registered representatives. Therefore, do not hesitate to ask brokers who are active in your stock for an introduction to the market-makers at their firms. Be prepared to visit with market-makers at least twice annually on a one-on-one basis and to invite them to visit your plant or facilities. A telephone call following a public announcement is also helpful.

After-market meetings for groups of market-makers should be held twice a year after the close of the trading day at a location convenient to the brokerage houses. Your market-makers should be encouraged to bring along any others who they feel might be interested in following the company and who could be influential in creating a fluid market for your securities.

Registered representatives are KSP-oriented. The better ones are analytically trained, but they still have to get a story across to their customers as succinctly as possible. Busy brokers find it difficult to break away from their telephones for luncheon meetings, but they should not be overlooked. After-market meetings and in some instances breakfast meetings are preferable for this audience.

Although inundated by invitations to meetings from public companies, analysts have the most flexibility in their daily schedules. The attention given a security analyst by a company management is repaid many times over if the result is a verbal endorsement or a market letter. The good analyst, however, is by nature a cynic. He has heard much, has been disappointed often, and is conservative in his expectations.

The analyst information portion of a financial public relations program requires great sensitivity. The analyst is half reporter and half accountant. By nature he is inquisitive and cynical, and should be. *Nelson's Directory* lists analysts by name and lists the companies and industries they have written about. This source and the *Financial Analysts Federation Directory* are invaluable tools. Begin by listing all the analysts who have written about your industry and your competitors; then telephone them to discuss your company. Follow up with a kit of material and an invitation to visit with you at your headquarters.

Be prepared to go to the office of any analyst who can't come to you. Periodic telephone updates will help bring the analyst closer to you. It is crucial that, within the full disclosure requirements, you candidly explain to the analyst all the negatives as well as the positives of your situation. Be prepared to discuss marketing plans in depth, product differentiation, and of course all the P&L reports and balance sheet ratios.

Analysts favor companies who are unafraid to discuss five-year programs. Although few companies can look back at a business plan five years later and claim they have met all the goals, analysts nonetheless want to be privy to your thinking.

Frequency of contact is an important element in a good financial relations program, and an annual or biannual visit to a community should be supplemented by telephone calls, one-on-one visits to those who are interested in sponsoring your stock, and the mailing of consequential literature. A flow of unimportant data will earn you the reputation of being a promoter; useful information, the reputation of being a quality manager.

A methodical system of reporting on conversations with brokers, analysts, and market-makers should be instituted. Important information flows from these sources, not only about market conditions that affect your securities but about competitors and their activities. Bear in mind that your own activities can be monitored by your competitors in the same way. Be certain that only a few executives are entrusted with the responsibility for speaking to brokers, analysts, and the press. Frequently, aggressive brokers call divisional executives whose names are listed in the annual report and attempt to get operating information.

The Press

With 45,000 publicly owned companies releasing information to the public, the business and financial press of the nation is inundated with news. The most important outlet for news is, obviously, *The Wall Street Journal* and the Dow Jones ticker; the criteria established by Dow Jones for the use of information eliminate many small companies. For instance, Dow Jones will not carry on its news wire or in *The Wall Street Journal* quarterly earnings of a company listed in the pink sheets. Transactions by all public companies of less than $3 million generally fail to make the Dow Jones ticker or *The Wall Street Journal,* and many smaller OTC companies do not engage in transactions or receive contracts with values of $3 million or more.

Two paid services, the Public Relations Newswire and the

Businesswire, have news machines placed strategically in news offices throughout the country and transmit news releases for a fee. These organizations also have news machines in selective brokerage offices, and their broker wires are useful in getting across a news story that might fail to be carried by Dow Jones.

A new service, The PR Newswire/OTC News Alert, transmits paid information to the desk-top computer terminals of many brokers and analysts. This service carries current news releases and a company profile that can be updated at any time. News releases are kept in the data bank for 90 days.

Most financial periodicals now offer a special section of "corporate news" — paid advertising, which readership studies show to be increasingly read.

Just as consumers are impressed more by third-party endorsements implicit in publicity articles than by advertising, so are shareholders, brokers, and analysts. Good publicity articles printed in local newspapers and trade magazines should be reprinted and sent to shareholders with the latest quarterly report and to market-makers, brokers, and securities analysts.

Good journalists normally number among their sources of information brokers and analysts who specialize in a particular industry or are known to cover a company or its technology. Brokers and analysts appreciate the visibility given them by managements who pass their names along to journalists doing a story on the company or its industry. A thoughtful public company executive will ask permission of those market-makers, brokers, and analysts who are especially knowledgeable about his company before giving their names to journalists.

Unless information must be disclosed immediately, it is unwise to release news on the day before a holiday or on a Friday afternoon. The later in the day a news item is released the more unlikely it becomes that it will run on the Dow Jones or Reuters wires, unless it is of great significance. The release of information by smaller companies or OTC companies before 9:30 A.M. EDT gives news editors the flexibility to use the item early on before the important news of the day begins to break or to slip it into the news flow during the day if there isn't a sufficient flow of major stories.

All press releases should carry an officer as the company contact. Dow Jones and Reuters always call to verify any news release. If the release relates to a talk before an analyst group, whether it be a formal analyst society meeting or an invitational group, a telephone number should be given for the site of the presentation, and a release should be disseminated before the speaker begins his talk. Timing of the distribution is delicate: If it is done prematurely and runs on the news wire, some of the invited guests might not attend; if it is released while the speaker is talking, an unwelcome telephone call might jar the presentation. The best solution we have found is to release some 30 minutes before the presentation, with a telephone call to the appropriate news desks to see if they want validation from the speaker before he begins.

In developing the publicity portion of the calendar, insert the four dates when press releases will be needed to report on quarterly or annual results. A fifth press release should be programmed for the annual meeting of shareholders. If the corporate official is in a position to project the year ahead, this can be widely publicized in the local and trade press and should also be directed at the editor of the "Annual Meeting's Briefs" column of *The Wall Street Journal.* These five "hard news" press releases should be supplemented by three or four feature-length publicity articles in either the trade or business press or a financial periodical. Of course, one can only work on developing articles with no guarantee of placing them, but a good publicity program will constantly ferret out angles of interest to investors. *Business Week,* for instance, has 12 departments, ranging from marketing to science and technology, each of them an opportunity for telling an unusual story about an aspect of your business. The purpose of slotting in objectives for feature stories is to remind the executive that he must be ever alert for opportunities to tell his company's story in greater detail than press release or hard news formats allow.

One must not overlook the excellent opportunities for publicity through cable television and business news broadcasts. Most major cities now have a dedicated local financial television channel, and these should be programmed into your 12-month calendar as supplements to the hard news and feature stories. Once you have successfully appeared on such a program, the tapes can serve as an audition and introduction to the producers of other financial programs in different regions of the country.

Shareholder Reports

Shareholders should receive quarterly reports from management even if the reporting is not mandated. These need not be expensive, but they must be attractive. Sometimes we forget that good graphics can make up for the lack of four colors. Good product photographs and easily read bar charts add to the usefulness of the document.

Nothing is as transparent as a president's message that dissembles. A bad year should be forthrightly discussed, and shareholders made aware of management's disappointment and the reasons for the poor performance.

The 10-K, which is extremely useful to the sophisticated investor, is less so to the uninitiated. Unless one wishes to discourage investor interest, a 10-K should not be a replacement for a printed shareholder report.

A technique much used in England but rarely in the United States is that of distributing product dividends to the shareholders. If one has a consumer item inexpensive enough to be sent along to the shareholder, doing so helps win shareholder loyalty. A movie chain, for example, could give shareholders a pair of free tickets at Christmas or some other occasions. As a large shareholder in a publicly owned record company for which we are not representatives, I have recently suggested that management each quarter send to all shareholders a sampler cassette of recordings that it will put on the marketplace in compact disc format in the following three months. This approach can also have a sales benefit for the company.

There are numerous other noncommunications techniques useful to shareholders and corporate management to develop and maximize interest in the company's shares and the value of the company's securities. The most obvious is a planned program of stock dividends.

Although most market professionals say that stock dividends are useless and sometimes inane, the truth is that shareholders love them. Indeed, stockbrokers and others begin to look forward to them once they have become a programmed event. A policy of issuing 3- to 5-percent stock dividends annually and making four-for-three or three-for-two stock splits in the $15–$20 stock range will win a company a larger following and ultimately a higher PE ratio.

Rarely does an OTC company, particularly a small one, have large attendance at its annual meeting of shareholders. As a result, shareholders in smaller companies who hear infrequently from management sell their holdings quickly on abrupt changes in price, either downward or upward. Clearly, the cost of generating a new shareholder is great, and while some fluidity in the market is essential to orderly trading, it is more beneficial that the core of shareholders be kept intact and friendly. With a financial community program in place, bringing management to key cities of the country, it might also be wise to consider invitations to local shareholders to attend a separate, informational meeting with management, devoted specifically to meeting management and answering shareholder questions. A simple note to local shareholders informing them that the CEO or CFO is going to be in town for several days and would welcome a visit and an opportunity to chat over cocktails could reap important benefits.

Special Events

Management should not overlook the inherent value to the financial community of trade shows and conferences. Analysts and brokers can be invited to the company's booth and given demonstrations of the product line. The event will also give analysts and brokers an opportunity to chat with potential buyers and develop a broader base of industry knowledge. If they are specialists in the industry, chances are the invitees will be attending the conference anyway. It is always helpful to secure a number of tickets to these shows and offer them to brokers and analysts who follow the company or the industry. If the conference hall offers facilities for meetings, a trade show is a good spot for a broker or analyst meeting.

Another important opportunity for investment support, this time from individual shareholders, is attendance and participation in the annual meetings of the National Association of Investment Clubs. A booth at one of these conferences will often generate 3,000 to 5,000 individual inquiries from members of clubs in the United States and overseas.

Merchandising and Remerchandising

We have spoken of the need to position a public company among shareholders in the same fashion that the marketing arm of the company positions its product line. In gaining attention and winning support, one must also merchandise and remerchandise the positive result of the financial public relations program. For instance, should a favorable trade magazine article or business item appear, it is in the interest of the company to mail a reprint to all shareholders, the company's bankers, the trade, and especially market-makers, brokers, and analysts. A market letter endorsing the securities of the company should be put in the press kit, but should not be sent to shareholders unless management is also willing to send out negative market letters. To take advantage of reprint information, the company should maintain an up-to-date mailing list, with each entry keyed so that it is easy to tell whether the person receiving literature is a market-maker, broker, analyst, money manager, banker, trade reporter, or local or financial journalist. As mailing lists build to large size, it is wise to clean the list annually by asking recipients if they want to continue on the list. By reviewing the names of those who either don't answer or ask to be dropped from the mailing list and analyzing their code identifications, one can quickly tell whether the communication program aimed at a specific audience is succeeding.

It is also wise to place your own name on the mailing list so that you can tell how long it takes for your literature to move through your public relations department into the field.

Public companies with consumer products have an interesting forum to exploit. If one is not squeamish, sales literature and display cartons can carry a variation of this notice: "ABC Corp., a publicly owned company whose shares are traded on the NASDAQ system under the symbol ABCX." An extension of this would include a similar message in trade or consumer advertisements and on the corporate letterhead.

It is also worth noting that foreign investors, particularly English and Scots, will invest in OTC U.S. securities and will hold these securities a very long time if given reason to do so. English and Scottish investors are generally patient and will invest long-term in companies with small capitalizations and modest revenues, if they are niche companies and leaders in their category. Should your company meet these qualifications and have unusual growth patterns, European markets are a possibility for future sponsorship. However, the approach to financial sponsorship just outlined must be adapted to specific market conditions in each country.

* * * * *

Donald Kirsch is one of the IR industry's founding practitioners. He has extensive experience as a corporate and agency IR executive and is respected nationally as an authority on IR for emerging corporations.

THE GOVERNMENT AFFAIRS PERSPECTIVE

Louis M. Thompson, Jr.
The National Investor Relations Institute

New York today is the undisputed financial capital of the world. Few, however, remember that the Big Apple was at one time a major political center. George Washington was sworn in as the first president of the United States, the first Congress met, and the Bill of Rights was adopted in New York.

Since those formative days of the United States, the political center of activity has clearly shifted to Washington, D.C., and so too has the center for the formation of policy affecting Wall Street and of financial policies affecting corporate America.

Investor relations, as opposed to pure public relations, is a regulated practice. And the laws that govern IR emanate from the U.S. Congress and state legislatures. Regulatory agencies such as the Securities and Exchange Commission and the Federal Reserve System translate these laws into regulations. Investor relations also answers to the self-regulatory organizations of the securities industry: The National Association of Securities Dealers and the various securities exchanges that regulate and monitor the activities of their members — securities dealers, firms, and listed companies.

In addition, each state has its securities laws, sometimes called "blue sky" laws, pertaining to the licensing of securities dealers, registration of securities offered for sale, pricing, and setting other terms for new issues.

Four years following the infamous stock market crash of 1929, Congress passed the Securities Act of 1933, creating the Securities and Exchange Commission, (founded on June 6, 1934). The SEC was given the oversight power to ensure that investors were given full and accurate information concerning securities offered for public sale and to prohibit fraud and misrepresentation in the sale of securities.

One year later, Congress passed the Securities Act of 1934, which gave Congress oversight authority for the securities exchanges and the practices of securities brokers and dealers. In 1938, the 1934 Act was amended to allow for the creation of the National Association of Securities Dealers, which, like the securities exchanges, is a self-regulatory body with considerable authority over the vast OTC market.

Congress has given the Board of Governors of the Federal Reserve System responsibility for regulating margin requirements for brokers and for setting rules for advancing credit to investors by lenders *other than* brokers and dealers in securities who are members of a national securities exchange. Such lenders might be, for example, commercial banks.

THE ROLE OF GOVERNMENT FROM THE IR PERSPECTIVE

These agencies and self-regulatory organizations (SROs) that oversee and regulate the activities of the securities industry and publicly traded companies provide the regulatory framework within which the IR executive operates. Although it is a framework of fairly well-defined laws and regulations, the interpretation of some regulations, particularly those related to disclosure, are sometimes less than precise.

Nevertheless, it is possible for an IR officer, once he or she becomes reasonably comfortable with the body of regulations, to view compliance with these rules as to the extent to which he or she needs to become involved with the regulatory or governmental aspects of IR. Today's top IR professionals are becoming more and more involved in the public-policy-making process that ultimately develops the laws and regulations under which they must operate. Public policy making that is the crux of this chapter.

Many corporations have executives with designated responsibility for government relations. In some instances where a senior vice president for corporate affairs has responsibility for IR, that same person also has the government relations function. Whatever the case, it is very important that IR and government relations be closely integrated in the management structure.

Congress does not consider legislation that directly impacts IR during every session, but when it does, the IR person must have the perspective necessary to evaluate the various ramifications of proposed legislation, understand how it would affect the corporation and its relations with shareowners, and interpret this to top management.

This necessity goes beyond consideration of state and federal legislation. It also includes awareness of proposals by special-interest groups, which could ultimately be brought before state and federal legislative bodies and become law. Some of those laws may be beneficial to corporations, some may not. But the time for the IR executive to take a role in this process *is during the formation period*. It is of little value to be on the sidelines and then complain about the enactment of bad law.

THE ROLE OF THE CONGRESS

The two major committees of Congress having oversight responsibility for the securities industry are the Senate Banking Committee and the House Energy and Commerce Committee. The Senate Banking Committee has a Securities Subcommittee with full-time professional staff members. On the House side, the Subcommittee on Consumer Protection, Telecommunications, and Finance handles securities issues and oversight of the SEC. It, too, has full-time staff members.

Following is a case that may illustrate how Congress relates to the securities industry and, more specifically, IR. In 1985, Congress passed a key bill called the Shareholder Communications Act of 1985. This piece of legislation actually had its beginnings in 1982 when the SEC Advisory Committee on Shareholder Communications held a series of hearings on ways to improve communication with shareholders. Representatives of the National Investor Relations Institute (NIRI) and other interest groups appeared before the SEC with their recommendations on how to improve this process.

One of the impediments to effective communication was determined to be the large number of shareholders whose stock was held in "nominee name" or "street name" accounts of brokerage firms or bank trust accounts. To the stock-issuing companies these were faceless, nameless accounts. The companies only knew that x number of shares were held, for example, by Merrill Lynch or by Manufacturers Hanover. Each proxy season, companies would send out search cards as of a record date, and the brokerage firm would request enough annual reports and proxies to cover their customers who held stock at the time in the requesting company. That number indicated how many of the people who owned stock in that company had accounts with the brokerage firm, but it would *not* tell how many shares they owned or who they were.

After input from NIRI and the issuing companies and considerable work with the SEC Advisory Committee on Shareholder Communication, the SEC recommended a system whereby beneficial owners of stock held in street name accounts could make their identity and number of share positions known to the issuing companies through an intermediary representing the brokerage firms or bank trust departments.

The SEC began the process of developing regulations that would amend Rule 14 of the Securities Act of 1934 (the Act giving it authority to regulate the activities of brokerage firms); the new regulations required all brokerage firms to survey their street name accounts (and subsequently do this on a request basis) to determine whether the individual account holders had any objection to their names, addresses, and numbers of shares be provided to the issuing companies.

However, while the SEC had regulatory authority over the brokerage firms, it did not have such authority over the banks and other financial services with custodial authority for trust accounts. Therefore, the SEC needed legislation bringing banks under its purview for shareholder communication purposes. Although that may sound simple, it was not. It therefore provides a good example of how the political system and policy process works and demonstrates the interrelationship among the SEC, the stock exchanges, and the interest groups representing the various factions of the securities industry.

The operational aspects of this whole regulatory process were directed by the New York Stock Exchange Ad Hoc Committee on Identification of Beneficial Owners. That committee comprised representatives of the New York Stock Exchange, the National Investor Relations Institute, the American Society of Corporate Securities, the Securities Industry Association, the American Bankers Association, and the Stock Transfer Association. The SEC provided a liaison person to work with the committee, and over a period of two years, the ad hoc committee worked out the system for the identification of "nonobjecting beneficial owners," or NOBOs, as they came to be known. The procedures worked out by the committee ultimately became the regulations that were issued by the SEC in the fall of 1985.

While this work was going on, the SEC, assisted primarily by the National Investor Relations Institute and the Securities Industry Association, sought legislation to give it rule-making authority over the banks for the purpose of shareholder communication.

At first the American Bankers Association objected to the SEC having this authority, since the banks were then regulated by the Comptroller of the Currency and the Federal Reserve System, and they did not want to deal with an additional regulatory agency. The ABA began a lobbying effort directed primarily at the two committees of the House and Senate that would have to approve the legislation before it went to the full Congress for a vote.

The ABA is one of the most powerful lobbying organizations in Washington, with a significant political action fund for contributing to members of Congress. Yet the arguments presented by the SEC, the NIRI, and the SIA for improved communication with those shareholders who had no objection to their identity being given to the issuing companies were so compelling that the bill passed the House Energy and Commerce Committee unanimously and was "polled" out of the Senate Banking Committee without objection. When brought to the floors of the House and Senate for passage, the bill passed by voice votes and was sent to the President for signature on December 28, 1985.

The ABA has since worked closely with the NYSE Ad Hoc Committee in developing the much more complicated procedures for identifying beneficial owners through the bank trust operations than was experienced with the brokerage firms. As of July 1, 1987, for the first time, there are regulations requiring the bank trust departments to process proxies and forward annual reports to their trust customers. The system will also greatly aid issuing companies in knowing who owns their stock and how many shares they have.

The shareholder communication rules also allow companies to communicate directly with those shareholders whose identities cannot be determined on a voluntary or nonobjecting basis.

At the end of 1986, one year after the regulations went into effect for the brokerage community, over 14 million individuals whose stock was held in nominee name accounts had no objection to being identified to the issuing companies. And, over 3,500 companies requested the lists of their NOBOs through the Independent Elections Corporation of America, the intermediary between the issuing companies and the brokerage houses or bank trust departments.

OTHER AREAS OF CONGRESSIONAL INTEREST

1987 was a watershed year for IR issues with governmental import. The record level of mergers and acquisitions, some of which were so-called hostile takeovers, brought calls from several sectors for legislation to curb the abuses of hostile takeovers. Sixteen CEOs of major American corporations paraded before the Senate Banking Committee on March 4, 1987, telling their stories of trying to govern their companies in an atmosphere where, any day, a hostile raider could put their companies into play with a minimum investment and play off the assets of the company in an effort to win control or take away huge profits in the form of "greenmail." Companies would take on heavy debt and pay the raiders a premium to buy back their stock to get them off their backs. Some of these companies had already experienced hostile takeover attempts. On the Democratic side of the two committees, the CEOs had a sympathetic ear. Some Republicans were also sympathetic. However, some of the free-market Republicans were opposed to any controls.

The insider trading scandal broke about the same time as the upsurge in hostile takeovers, and many on Capitol Hill and elsewhere were looking for the connection between the two issues. The SEC's Enforcement Division in conjunction with the U.S. District Attorney's office for the Southern District of New York cracked down on insider trading activities. A series of hearings was held before the Senate Banking Committee and the House Energy and Commerce Committee on their respective bills addressing takeovers and insider trading.

The three major bills being considered each had significant IR implications. For each bill, executives needed to ensure that their companies' government relations people knew what to lobby for or against. In the course of considering this legislation, the two major committees heard testimony from investment bankers, corporate CEOs, lawyers who specialized in takeovers, and special-interest groups, such as T. Boone Picken's United Shareholders of America. They were opposed to the legislation, saying the bills favored CEOs trying to preserve their jobs against the interest of shareholders.

As in any legislative situation, where both sides can get emotional over an issue, the chances for a truly good bill that will benefit society as a whole are somewhat slim. Those with the loudest voices who can make the best presentation of their case tend to prevail.

The conditions were right for this legislation, and the various special interests were organized to make their case before Congress. The IR impact may well be felt for years to come.

THE ROLE OF SPECIAL-INTEREST GROUPS

Special-interest groups play a significant role in the public policy process. The perception that legislation is a creation of Congress or state legislatures clouds what really happens. It is true that Congress plays a major role in setting legislative priorities and writing legislation, but the ideas behind the bills come in large part from the many interest groups competing for the attention of Congress — in particular, of the professionals who staff the committees.

Trade associations, professional associations, consumer groups, individual corporations, and individual citizens are just part of the body politic that influences the legislative process. Some groups go to Congress year after year with a legislative agenda representing their particular interests. Some take a stand on issues when the need arises. Issues affecting IR occur more often in the latter context.

It is not every year that hostile takeovers or insider trading, for example, dominates the scene. And it is more difficult for interest groups, under these circumstances, to compete for attention when they are not an ever-present part of the political scene on Capitol Hill. It takes more effort and skill to organize the "grass roots" support of their members to push for legislation, and the issues themselves have to be clearly defined, studied, documented, and presented to gain the attention of legislative decision makers. But it can be done.

Who are some of the players in the securities area? The Securities Industry Association, the National Association of Securities Dealers, the stock exchanges, the National Investor Relations Institute, the American Bankers Association, the American Society of Corporate Secretaries, the American Institute of Certified Public Accountants, the American Finance Association, the Association of Investment Bankers, the Financial Executives Institute, the National Association of Investors Corporation, the National Security Traders Association, the Financial Analysts Federation and its local societies, the United Shareholders Association, the Investor Responsibility Research Center, and the American Association of Individual Investors all make up special-interest groups representing the investment community.

Do these groups work together for a common purpose? The answer is that some do, but most address an issue from a special-interest perspective. Sometimes they have competing interests and can wage significant battles over a bill. These groups have dues paying members and professional staffs, many of which are headquartered in Washington, D.C., or New York City. Some are staffed with professionals in the legislative arena backed by significant political action funds. Others get into legislation or regulatory issues when the need arises but do not have large lobbying staffs or the political funding that is sometimes necessary to get legislators' attention. The bottom line is that legislative clout varies considerably, and that variation can have a major impact on the outcome.

What is interesting, from an IR point of view, is that with an estimated 47 million individual investors and many more indirect investors through pension funds, there is no single interest group that can claim this major grass-roots potential as its members. The American Association of Individual Investors, for example, claims 100,000 members, 0.2 percent of the total. The United Shareholder Association claims 12,000.

HOW THE PROCESS WORKS

In 1987, the Investor Responsibility Research Center, a Ralph Nader–spawned organization founded in 1972, conducted a study on the proxy process. The study was funded by the United Shareholders Association, an organization founded by T. Boone Pickens.

The IRRC was founded as an information service "for institutional shareholders who wish to make independent assessments of the policies of their portfolio companies."[1] The IRRC has since become active in the areas of corporate governance, South Africa divestment, energy, and defense. It also works closely with the Council of Institutional Investors, which

---

[1] 1986 Annual Report. Investor Responsibility Research Center. Washington, D.C.

represents many of the nation's largest public pension funds (members' holdings are some $200 billion).

The IRRC study concluded that:

> The voting system is not working as it should. The voting system is dominated by corporate management, which has a strong vested interest in the outcome of controversial or contested items that are put to a shareholder vote. Institutional investors, a potential check on corporate management, face serious conflicts of interest in voting, and many institutions have succumbed to management pressures to support voting proposals that are not in shareholders' interests. Management proposals that are contrary to shareholders' interest are passing overwhelmingly, even at companies that have high levels of institutional ownership. The voting process itself, which has become extraordinarily complex as a result of the nominee registration system that is used to register most securities today, is vulnerable to fraud.[2]

T. Boone Pickens sent a letter on July 2, 1987, to members of the United Shareholders Associations (USA) asking them:

> to write key officials in Washington to demand confidential proxy voting. The overwhelming evidence shows that corporations blatantly abuse the proxy process and that it is susceptible to fraud.
>
> Corporate elections are the only elections in America where the incumbents make out the ballots, count the votes, and tell the voters how it turned out. Not only does management see how each shareholder voted, but they also use shareholders' money to try to change the votes they don't like. In a system like that, it's virtually impossible for owners to prevail.

Mr. Pickens' letter also included "talking points," such as the fact that a survey conducted by the New York Society of Security Analysts showed 75 percent favored confidentiality in shareholder voting.

Since the SEC regulates the proxy process, the IRRC and the USA are aiming their effort both at the SEC — to step up its enforcement of regulations already on the books — and at Congress — to write new legislation to deal with the problems outlined.

---

[2] Executive Summary, "Conflicts of Interest in the Proxy Voting System," by James E. Heard and Howard D. Sherman. Investor Responsibility Research Center. Washington, D.C., 1987

The proxy issue is wrapped in the rhetoric of corporate governance — who owns and who governs the corporation. Corporate managers increasingly complain that it is difficult to manage their companies for the long-term interests of the corporation and its shareowners when the institutional investors are generally more interested in short-term results. When the 16 CEOs testified before the Senate Banking Committee in March 1987 on takeover legislation, a number of them discussed the problem of managing in a short-term environment. With institutional investors holding a greater percentage of stock and conducting some 80 percent of the daily trading activity, the role of the institutional investor has become very important to the corporation and to the IR executive.

The adage that investors who did not like what a corporation was doing could "vote with their feet" (sell the stock), is in many cases no longer applicable. Some institutional investors have such large positions that they cannot easily pull out and have, therefore, decided to take a more active role in corporate governance.

Although is not yet settled, it is possible to speculate with some confidence that the Council of Institutional Investors and the United Shareholders Association, backed by the studies of the Investor Responsibility Research Center, will attempt to get the attention of the Senate Banking and the House Energy and Commerce Committees and to persuade their interested subcommittees to hold hearings on the proxy issue. If these groups can muster sufficient support, they will probably work with the committee staffs in writing a bill that seeks to deal with the problems as they see them.

Interest groups representing the corporations will probably be called on to testify at the hearings, and they too will try to influence the drafting of the legislation, or perhaps to get a member or members of Congress to sponsor a bill representing the interests of the corporations.

If the corporations, represented by their associations, decide to oppose a proxy bill, then they will try to muster support to kill the bill while it is still in committee. If that fails, they will have to launch a much greater effort to get sufficient votes to stop the legislation should it come to a vote before the full House or Senate.

Corporations represent a major grass-roots constituency that often is not used to its potential. That constituency is comprised of shareowners, employees, customers, suppliers, and members of the communities in which the corporations have plant operations.

Each of these constituents reside or operate in a congressional district and a state with two U.S. senators. A major company with operations in a number of locations throughout the country can muster considerable political clout.

THE ROLE OF THE IR EXECUTIVE

The IR officer can start by recognizing that what takes place in the evolution of public policy, resulting in legislation and regulations affecting the corporation, is part of his or her job responsibility. While the actual lobbying may be done by the government relations executive, staying abreast of developments that have IR import, and advising management accordingly, should be part of an IR job description.

This can be done by monitoring the financial press, publications such as the *SEC Docket* or other newsletters reporting on SEC activities, and the *Federal Register;* by subscribing to one of the "on-line" legislative monitoring services; or by assigning these functions to consultants. The National Investor Relations Institute assists its members in this process by publishing the *NIRI Washington Alert,* which tells them what issues are coming up and what kind of response is appropriate.

Since the introduction of legislation affecting IR is not an everyday occurrence, it will probably take some extra effort to consider monitoring this as part of one's job. And, if one perceives his or her job as being primarily an analyst contact for the company and doesn't see the broader scope of IR, it will be even more difficult. Yet, if the IR person does not do it, the opportunity for the corporation to have an impact on the public policy process could be lost.

There is also no question that involvement in governmental issues is becoming a definite point of consideration in the more senior-level IR positions, particularly those involving the full spectrum of corporation relations.

CONCLUSION

Although the IR practitioner is not going to place the regulatory/government relations aspects among the higher job priorities, being aware of the implications and consequences is extremely important. Having the ability to understand the relationship of these issues to the IR function and to management of the company will not only distinguish one's performance, but will have a measurable impact on the public policy process.

*   *   *   *   *

Louis M. Thompson, Jr., is president of the National Investor Relations Institute. He was assistant White House press secretary for President Ford and senior military assistant to the Assistant Secretary of Defense for Public Affairs.

WHY IT'S IMPORTANT TO UNDERSTAND WHO OWNS STOCK

Robert Ferris
Doremus Porter Novelli

In today's dynamic financial marketplace, leading companies recognize that IR is the vehicle through which they market their most important product, namely, the company itself. In this chapter we address the importance of assessing current equity ownership and interest. This information plays a critical role in the effective management of IR and in the development of the IR marketing plan. (There is applicability in debt holder relations, as well, but we will concentrate here on equity IR efforts as they are more prevalent.)

In view of the increased competition for investment dollars and market "sponsorship," beneficial ownership analysis makes good marketing sense. Unfortunately, however, the tendency has been to view stock watching only as a means of protection or corporate survival. In other words, "If it isn't done, some corporate raider might launch a surprise attack on my company." There certainly should be a broader mindset to such analyses.

To be sure, ownership analysis is important to the strategic IR manager for at least five key reasons:

- It is a primary market research tool for a proactive IR program.
- It provides a logical source of information about investor perceptions.

- It is a logical resource for additional capital financings.
- It provides a useful reference in gauging pass or fail expectations of management stockholder proposals.
- It can spell the difference between success or failure in maintaining corporate control.

MARKET RESEARCH

The primary reason for understanding stock ownership is that the ongoing process analysis is the IR manager's best market research tool. Knowing who current stockholders are and having ready information to target potential stockholders from a review of peer ownership provides efficiency to the process of screening a market universe that is increasingly veiled and dispersed throughout the world.

The IR manager has a host of investment influentials (as well as investors themselves) from which to devise a marketing strategy. The playing field is the globe, with pension fund investors, alone, accounting for trillions of investable dollars. In addition, the IR manager can access many other investing institutions directly, plus investment intermediaries, brokerage analysts, money managers, as well as the retail market of individual investors.

Where does one start? Where can the IR manager get the best return on the investment of time and budget? The stockholder list provides many of the obvious answers and the direction. Of course, the IR manager should ferret out the beneficial interest behind record ownership positions, with emphasis on the meaningful positions. Information, such as the identity of the institution itself, the buy-side (institutional) analyst, the sell-side (brokerage) analyst who sells research on your company to that investor, the voting and investment discretion of the broker or bank trust officer involved with that particular account — such market intelligence is critical (and obvious) to effective IR management.

Since as a general rule securities are sold, not bought, it is incumbent that public companies understand who the buyers are and continue to nurture their respective aftermarkets with information, corporate perspective, and encouragement. The IR manager marshals the effort most efficiently by knowing the most likely targets of interest.

Market research is a multifaceted evolution for the IR manager. While the ultimate measurement of IR success is the highest multiple of earnings one could expect to attain given an "informed market," development of interest, credibility, sponsorship, and investment is a long-term, never-ending process.

How do you know your strategies are working? How do you obtain "signals" of areas needing improvement? Ask interested parties. They'll tell you. And the most interested parties are those who own you or those who influence the market for your securities. They provide the IR manager with "intelligence" on corporate communications effectiveness, investment merit, industry and company-specific critical issues, etc. — intelligence that helps the IR manager focus strategy and support the business and financial goals of the company. This is another good reason for ownership analysis.

OWNERS — A FUNDING SOURCE

Investment relations managers have played an increasingly important role in corporate capital funding efforts, complementing the efforts of the finance department. With a good fix on current beneficial ownership make-up, as well as on those market influentials (brokerage houses, sell-side analysts, etc.) that have been active in, or supporting the stock, the IR manager can direct the creation of an underwriting group in syndicated offerings and can also help direct the selling effort toward a more logical investor audience. Of course, since the IR manager contrasts ownership against peer ownership, the target investor group can expand in a significant, logical fashion.

The more intelligence the company has, in terms of existing ownership and interests, the better it is positioned to "manage" its financings, with the help of its bankers.

CAN PROPOSALS THAT HELP MANAGEMENT WIN PROXY SUPPORT?

The rise in institutional and special-interest investor activism and associated corporate governance issues and strategies is a subject of increasing concern and corporate attention. Many companies have been updating their by-laws, recasting their charters to allow management and the board more corporate flexibility and to provide mechanisms to address governance as well as new financing issues. The merit of such activity is not a matter for discussion in this chapter, but it is important to understand that such changes or amendments require stockholder approval, many in super-majority measure.

During the process of ownership analysis, independent of or incident to the annual proxy solicitation process, the IR manager should learn where voting control rests, as well as identifying any proxy committee disposition or policy toward various "governance" or "corporate control" issues. Such critical information from ownership analysis can signal whether management can expect to gain the requisite stockholder support for its proposals — indeed, whether a proposal should be made or not.

Recently, the preoccupation with trading activity by potential raiders has resulted in a surfeit of products and services designed to help companies analyze stock lists. By focusing on such "quick hit" or "alert" methodologies, however, the IR manager will probably not find what he is looking for. The IR manager is more apt to discern unusual activity or accumulations through ongoing market analysis efforts, whether in discussion with investment influentials or through tracking large block purchases. The fact is, however, that today's corporate raiders are happy to make their stock ownership publicly known in order to pressure a board of directors to listen to proposals or to affect the value of the company's shares by putting the company in "play" and thus obtain a better buy-out price.

The "quick fix" that such stock-watching products and services offer is not a replacement for the kind of market intelligence that true stockholder analysis should entail. The fragmented pieces of information an IR manager obtains from these analyses of transfer sheets, 13-F reports, depository position listings, etc., will be useless to the IR manager without a proactive approach in communicating with investors.

MECHANICS OF OWNERSHIP ANALYSIS

In this respect, there is no better way to discern ownership than to ask. The answers the IR manager receives will place the fragments of owner information he already has into a valid context.

By turning attention away from myopic concerns about potential corporate hostilities and toward the real value of stock ownership analysis, the IR manager will better serve the needs of the company — and be in a better contingency posture, to boot. Stock ownership analysis as a market research tool provides the efficiency needed to communicate with today's important shareholders.

Fundamental to the IR manager's ownership analysis is the 13-F ownership report. With these listings, the IR manager is able to identify the major institutional shareholders of the company and those of comparable companies. By identifying these shareholders, the IR manager can develop a network of information sources.

Another important information-gleaning tactic is talking to sell-side analysts. These analysts know quite a lot about investment interest — who's buying, who's selling, rumors in the marketplace, etc. Obviously intelligence on buying interest provides a far more valuable perspective than that on selling interest.

Important information can also be gained through the annual meeting solicitation process. In regular meeting situations, actual proxy solicitation might not always be necessary. However, it is a useful tool for obtaining additional insights on ownership, e.g., type of institutional owner, the number of accounts behind a consolidated position, and the name of key contacts on proxy committees. It is certainly recommended that companies occasionally use the services of a professional proxy solicitor for regular annual meetings; these services are, of course, of paramount importance when material proposals are included in the agenda (which may or may not require super-majority stockholder vote).

As the information obtained from annual meeting solicitations is a valuable component to the market research effort, it might be wise for IR managers to consider conducting a "proxy search" twice a year. This would provide midyear updates of information about the number of accounts behind "street-name" positions, which is very helpful in suggesting a more targeted plan of action for the IR manager. It also provides continuing, current insight into investment trends among banks and brokerage firms.

Also, it is always possible to ask banks and brokers with large positions in the company's stock for account breakouts. The IR manager can find out about geographic concentrations of interest, social demographics, account numbers, and position ranges. As this information is becoming more and more valuable, many banks and brokerages are charging a nominal access fee, but the information is usually worth the cost.

As we stated earlier, 13-F filings are the most productive source of ready information. These listings should cover most of the company's largest owners. By following up with analysts at these institutions as well as using other readily available reference sources, such as the *Mutual Fund Directory,* IR managers can discover who the custodians for these positions are and correlate this information with the list of holders of record, an additional help in identifying beneficial owners. Information provided in 13-F listings also helps to define areas of current activity, making it easier to target key audiences for further inquiries and investor communications efforts.

In addition, 13-F reports indicate voting control and investment authority. Obviously, this information is a matter of public record, so it is advisable that the IR manager obtain 13-F reports on peer group companies, as it will provide the best source of prospective investors, adding to program (time/budget) efficiency in new outreach efforts.

It should be noted that 13-F information is neither complete nor timely (only managers of $100 million in assets or more are required to report, and most of the information is more than 45 days old when it becomes available), but it is a good enough beginning to ownership analysis. We would like to see better SEC policing of filings as we believe it would not only encourage more institutions to file but also encourage them to file more promptly after the end of the quarter.

Another useful source is the depository breakdown. While the advent of the Depository Trust Company in the early 70s further clouded the identity of stockholders, it certainly has provided for more efficient administration of the proxy process than brokerage and bank back office proxy operations.

Position reports from CEDE (Depository Trust Company), KRAY, PACIFIC, PHILADEP and other depositories can be used to trace current trading activity between depository members (banks and brokerages). The vast majority of trading volume for most companies will pass through the depository. In fact, CEDE is the largest single stockholder of record for most listed public companies.

One benefit of the information received is that, in identifying a brokerage firm's retail interest in the company, the IR manager can blanket its brokers with useful background information to encourage and maintain their interest and perhaps additional investment. The focus can be narrowed, geographically, through closer analysis.

Most companies should consider looking at depository listings (particularly CEDE) on a monthly basis. For more actively traded companies, a weekly review, showing day-to-day transfers, will provide a most useful perspective.

Although we stress the need to question investors directly, it is important to point out that their responses will vary greatly depending on their own priorities. Some investors, for example, are more likely to respond to an ownership inquiry directly from the issuer. This is particularly true in Europe, where investors are wary of outside agents. In fact, nowadays European investors are more likely to respond to an inquiry regarding investment interest, ownership, and interest in meeting with management than their American counterparts. Dealing directly with the issuer also appeals to the egos of many investors.

Ownership inquiries can be conducted through telephone survey, but the most effective approach is the one-on-one meeting with the IR manager and periodical meetings with the company's top management. By defining what kind of investor is interested in the company, the IR manager can develop a direct (sales) effort that most directly reaches the target audience. Interest on the part of one European fund manager is an indication that the company may interest others. If the majority of the company's shareholders are retail and the float is thin, then perhaps an IR program devoted to institutions will not reach the appropriate investor base, or perhaps the program is oriented too exclusively to retail investors and needs to focus more on institutions.

The active involvement of the IR manager in one-on-one efforts is vital. Armed with an understanding of the economies of the business, he must have both the analytical skills to address accounting and financial fundamentals and strong communications skills to interest the audience. By talking regularly to the company's (listed) stock specialists or (NASDAQ) market-makers, an IR manager can gain invaluable information on interest in the company. Regular contact is the key. However, remember to use contacts judiciously. It can be a death blow to networking efforts to wear out the welcome.

In addition to an active IR manager, it is important to involve the chief executive officer and chief financial officer in the intelligence networking effort. They are often aware of institutional ownership information through their business and social contacts, as are members of the board of directors.

The IR manager, however, must ensure that he is the central repository of information. By encouraging the CEO, CFO, and board members to provide acquired market intelligence on the company, the IR manager is in an excellent position to provide a credible, comprehensive situation analysis to top management and the board. Such formal reports are recommended quarterly and should address all matters of market intelligence, from ownership to valuation analysis to comparative stock price performance and trading patterns to investor perceptions of investment merit and concern, all of which are integral to the company's strategic planning process.

I trust you can see that the value of ownership analysis extends far beyond its serving the company's interests in contested situations. The success or failure of management and the board regarding its fiduciary duty in bids for control does not rest on its ability to detect unusual accumulations in the stockholder list. In such cases it is much more important for management to be able to use its time wisely in responding after the bell goes off. With the limited time available to management to respond to a hostile takeover or a friendly overture, carefully developed shareholder intelligence gives the company the capability to more effectively and efficiently, in everyone's best interest.

By paying less attention to trading activity on the part of potential corporate raiders and more attention to the fundamental benefits of ownership analysis, the IR manager will be able to help shape long-term strategies that enhance value, and thus lessen the threat of hostilities.

* * * * *

Robert D. Ferris is senior vice president of Doremus Porter Novelli.

THE ROLE OF INVESTOR RELATIONS IN HOSTILE TAKEOVER BIDS

Richard E. Cheney and Edward O. Raynolds
Hill and Knowlton, Inc.

Today's takeover climate is marked by fast-played sequences of moves and countermoves; megabuck bids, poison pills, and other arcane defenses; arbitrageurs who take billion-dollar stock positions; tricks bag of legal maneuvers; and frantic efforts by investment bankers to line up preemptive transactions.

In this succession of seeming life-and-death strokes, is there a place for the investor communications function?

It's true that the role of IR/public relations in takeovers often is not as dominant as it once was. Nevertheless, good, innovative investor communications is still essential in a struggle for control. Many times, it will swing the balance.

Consider the well-known Marathon-Mobil struggle. Writing about the influence of public relations on that fight's outcome, *The Wall Street Journal* said:

> Marathon quickly buttressed its legal strengths with a highly effective public relations campaign. Like a jujitsu wrestler, Marathon used Mobil's weight against it by harping on Mobil's size, its well-known desire to obtain oil cheaply, its high public profile and its perceived "to-hell-with-them-all" attitude. ...Mobil's legions of experts may appear to have been splendidly equipped to fight a public relations battle, but Marathon's guerrilla campaign was highly effective.

> In fact, a careful reading of the judicial opinions in the court cases, combined with discussions with court officials, clearly indicate that Marathon's public relations campaign strongly influ-

enced the court proceedings. To an unusual degree, social issues were incorporated in judicial decisions.

The contest was resolved in 1982, when Marathon was able to complete a friendly merger with U.S. Steel. While the fight was ostensibly settled on a legal basis, it is clear that Marathon's effective public relations effort helped create a climate in which events unfolded in the company's favor.

In this chapter, we will examine some of the basic ways in which the IR/public relations function plays a key role in a takeover situation. We will then look at some of the kinds of communications strategies that can be employed in takeovers, and review some instances in which these strategies were employed.

BEGIN WHILE THE WATER'S CALM

The IR function must go to work long before a takeover is on the horizon. A stock whose value fails to reflect a company's worth will be one that winds up on the raider's computer screen.

If the company's financial relations program is failing to get the company's strengths and future direction across to investors, a takeover bid will be all the more likely. There is much truth to the adage: "The best defense against a takeover is a good financial public relations program."

Take the case of a large pharmaceutical–consumer products company. It did such an effective job of restructuring — and of communicating the benefits of that restructuring — that a major business magazine wrote that the company's enhanced market valuation had placed it out of range for a potential acquisitor.

BYLAW AND CHARTER CHANGES: TEST THE WATERS

Many companies today have adopted changes to their by-laws or amendments to their charters to prevent or slow down a hostile takeover attempt. But shareholders may refuse to adopt antitakeover proposals submitted for their vote. If so, a raider may interpret this action as an invitation from shareholders to make an offer.

Large institutional shareholders have opposed many such measures vociferously, sometimes taking a public position against a charter amendment a large company has proposed. Faced with this kind of resistance, many companies now test the waters before actually proposing charter amendments, in order to determine institutional shareholders' reactions. A competent proxy solicitation firm can poll institutional holders to learn their attitudes on a certain kind of measure without revealing the name of the company that plans to propose it.

Companies are also taking extra care to presell sensitive proposals to institutional holders. Management and institutions often meet face-to-face to review the reasons for such proposals and thereby increase the likelihood of a favorable vote.

Another useful step for a company is to inform its board of directors about the true nature of their responsibilities in a takeover situation. Management wants to be sure that the board is prepared to act promptly and decisively and that it is not afraid to take a position that seems to support management — when that position is also in the best interests of the company's shareholders.

MEDIA RELATIONS: START NOW

How can investor communications prepare for a takeover bid, if and when one occurs?

It's no secret that the market runs on information, and the news media are key providers of that information. The quality of a company's relations with the media, then, will be the critical factor in a takeover situation. A company who has stiff-armed the media for years will come into a takeover fray with a serious handicap — especially if its adversary has worked carefully to cultivate press favor.

But a company with good media relations already has a leg up on beating an unwanted offer. When Sun made a bid for Becton, Dickinson in 1978, Becton was able to generate major stories advancing its viewpoint, due to the fine media relations it had established.

KNOW YOUR OWNERS

One key to being on guard for a hostile move against your company is knowing who your owners are. Hill and Knowlton, as well as some other firms, has a stock-watch function in place that tracks trading activity and unusual buy-sell interest on minute-by-minute basis. This service provides a quick focus on unusual trading, giving a company an early warning to suspicious share accumulations.

Stock watch works hand-in-hand with an ownership analysis program that gets behind street name holdings and bank nominee names. This effort not only flags questionable share positions, but supports the IR effort by providing a timely opportunity to identify and contact new holders of the company's securities.

ORGANIZE IN ADVANCE

A decade or so ago, companies used to compile "black books" listing all steps they would take to repel any hostile offer that surfaced. Since then, court decisions have underscored managements' and directors' obligations to act in shareholders' best interests. These rulings have made the black book extinct. Today, a company can be sued successfully if it takes an attitude of rejecting any takeover bid out-of-hand before determining whether the offer benefits its shareholders.

That is not to say that a company should not have procedures in place for dealing with an unsolicited takeover bid — so long as those procedures don't violate the principle of placing shareholder interests first. These steps are largely organizational, and they include

• *Designating a project manager for the fight effort,* usually someone at a high management level reporting directly to the CEO.

• *Establishing responsibilities and a structure* for dealing with the many kinds of calls and inquiries the company will receive from the news media, investment community, shareholders, and arbitrageurs. The number of these calls can be overwhelming.

Often, additional help, such as that of outside financial public relations specialists, should be enlisted.

• *Setting up a system for monitoring the news coverage* that a potential fight will generate, and a system to distribute clippings and wire dispatches to all members of the fight team — often including monitoring over weekends and holidays.

• *Preparing lists of news media to be reached,* nationally and locally, together with their deadlines. This step will be critical to deciding how and when to release news. Note that the amount and depth of news coverage of an event diminish as deadlines draw closer. The earlier in the day news can be announced, the better.

• *Assembling the names of leaders of key constituent groups,* such as employees and unions, local communities groups, customers and suppliers, legislators, and politicians. These constituent leaders should be kept continuously apprised of developments. In a contested bid, companies may find it extremely useful to enlist their support. (See "Communications' Strategy Role," below.)

• *Gathering the advertising deadlines* of relevant national and local newspapers, and establishing a system for clearing and placing any ads that might be produced in a fight.

• *Having managers sign off on a disclosure/information handling/stock trading policy* to assure the company has taken adequate steps to prevent the misappropriation of information or insider trading. This kind of policy is all the more important in the wake of insider trading scandals that have rocked Wall Street.

THE COMMUNICATIONS PERSON SHOULD HAVE A KEY ROLE

When a company receives an unsolicited bid, the IR or public relations person should be sitting at the strategy table with the investment bankers, lawyers, and proxy solicitors. All these key players will have experience, contacts, and familiarity with the most recent strategies, as well as knowledge of the bidder

An effective investor communications specialist knows the rules, understands the role of other team members, and knows what the media consider newsworthy. The communication specialist may also have the resources to achieve results in any part of the country or world on short notice.

The communications officer will also know local media contacts. He is generally sensitive to employee concerns and has a firm knowledge of the industry. Most takeover struggles leave a residue of damage that public relations must address. In many cases, the in-house communications officer can suggest ways to mitigate serious damage as the contest progresses.

HANDLING THE TASK

In a takeover struggle, dozens of press releases must be prepared, cleared, and distributed. Basic announcements include the commencement of the offer, litigation, court decisions, end of a proration period, Hart-Scott-Rodino developments, charges, countercharges, etc. Often, companies need to issue more than one release on a single day.

Having a well-organized, well-equipped, and well-coordinated communications organization in place to handle such an effort is essential. Often, a company's internal communications department is very good at disseminating ongoing company news. But in the heat of a takeover battle, it sometimes lacks the resources or experience to deal with lawyers and investment bankers as effectively as it needs to. As noted above, outside specialists may be useful.

Seizing the initiative in takeover communications is essential, since the first announcements of a takeover shape investors' perceptions.

STOP, LOOK, AND LISTEN

When a company receives an unsolicited takeover bid, it usually is not ready to take a position either for or against the offer. Typically, the company will wait until it can assemble its board of directors, who must carefully consider whether the bid is in shareholders' interests before recommending acceptance or rejection.

That does not mean a company must be silent until it can convene a directors' meeting. Investors may interpret silence at this stage as confusion or disarray. Rule 14a-9 of the Securities and Exchange Commission permits a company to make a statement that takes a position neither for nor against a takeover offer, but simply states that the company has received the offer, is considering it, and will advise shareholders of its position at a later time.

This communication usually takes the form of a short letter to shareholders, called a "Stop, Look, and Listen Letter." The company generally incorporates the gist of the letter in a news release for general distribution:

SAFEWAY STORES COMMENTS ON DART GROUP TENDER OFFER

Oakland, CA, July 9, 1986 — Safeway Stores Inc. (NYSE; SA) said that its board of directors, together with its independent financial and legal advisors, Merrill Lynch Capital Markets and Wachtell, Lipton, Rosen & Katz, will evaluate carefully and thoroughly the unsolicited $58-a-share tender offer commenced today by a subsidiary of Dart Group Corp. and will make a recommendation to shareholders by July 22.

The company said it has instructed its advisors to commence immediately their review and analysis of the financial and legal aspects of Dart's offer.

Safeway asked its shareholders to take no action with respect to their shares until the company announces its recommendation.

HAMMERMILL DIRECTORS WILL STUDY TENDER OFFER

Erie, Pa., July 27, 1986 — W. Craig McClelland, president and chief executive officer of Hammermill Paper Co., said today in response to the unsolicited and conditional $52-per-share tender offer for all of Hammermill's outstanding common shares:

"Hammermill's board of directors will carefully study the offer and consult with its outside legal and financial advisors. After doing so, we will advise shareholders of our conclusion and recommendations. We will make our views known no later than August 7, 1986, and hopefully, sooner. In the interim, there is no need for Hammermill shareholders to take any action with respect to the offer."

T-BAR RECEIVES TENDER OFFER

Wilton, CT, Oct. 30, 1986 — T-Bar Inc. (AMEX: TBR) today advised shareholders that a wholly owned subsidiary of John Beall & Company, Inc. had commenced an unsolicited and conditional tender offer for the common shares of T-Bar at $7.25 per share.

Beall has also tendered for T-Bar's convertible subordinated debentures.

The company said that the board of directors has retained Kidder Peabody & Co., Inc. and Needham & Co., Inc. as its financial advisors and Skadden Arps Slate Meagher & Flom as legal advisors to assist in the evaluation of the offer.

T-Bar said its board will review the offer in due course and will make a recommendation to shareholders. T-Bar urged shareholders not to take any action with respect to the offer until T-Bar's board had made its recommendation.

DIAMOND SHAMROCK TO REVIEW
MESA UNSOLICITED OFFER

Dallas, Jan. 7, 1987 — The unsolicited tender offer announced today by a partnership composed of affiliates of Mesa Limited Partnership and Harbert Corp. for up to 20 million Diamond Shamrock common shares at $15 a share in cash is under consideration by Diamond Shamrock's board and management.

Following evaluation of the unsolicited offer, in consultation with its legal and financial advisers, the board will make its recommendation to stockholders promptly, and in any event by Jan. 20. Until that time, Diamond Shamrock requests that all stockholders refrain from accepting or rejecting the offer.

REJECTING AN OFFER

Once the target company's board of directors meets, it may vote to reject the unsolicited offer. If so, the company will want to issue a second release advising investors of the board's action.

This kind of release frequently states that the company is exploring alternatives other than the bid it has received, in order to enhance shareholder value.

WORKING WITH THE MEDIA

If the company is the one making the offer, it will want to immediately provide the media with information about itself. The first story will report the terms of the offer. On either the same day or the next, the press will usually publish stories giving an analysis of what the combined companies would look like, assuming the takeover is successful. The media prepare these stories based on previously published company materials, available research reports, and reports of conversations with security analysts familiar with both companies.

The communications team should help reporters by making company material available and by providing the names of analysts who are familiar with the company. Obviously, it is beneficial to identify analysts who appreciate the values the company is building as a continuing concern.

There are times in a fight when a company will wish to — or be forced to — say nothing. A seasoned communications specialist knows how to say "No comment" to reporters without turning them off in a way that will hurt the company later on.

INFORMING PROFESSIONAL INVESTORS

Getting material effectively into the hands of professional investors also can have a significant effect on news coverage. This is so because financial journalists rely heavily on investment professionals to interpret company and industry situations, and they often quote analysts in their stories.

It is very effective, particularly for a bidder at the outset of a takeover contest, to send a complete package of material to all potentially interested security analysts. Not only do the analysts then have complete information in hand to advise clients on how to respond to the takeover, but they are well-informed when the media calls them for comment.

SHAREHOLDER LETTERS, ADVERTISEMENTS

There are two major vehicles for accomplishing takeovers, the tender offer and the proxy fight. In the real world, struggles for control often take on strange shapes, so that a given takeover effort technically may involve neither or both of these two vehicles.

In any case, a takeover contest often involves direct communications with the shareholders of the sought-after company. These communications are usually letters. What they are allowed to say, as well as the rules for obtaining government clearance for them, are set forth by the SEC.

These communications letters usually take on a second form — as a news release — and sometimes a third form — as a paid advertisement.

Although costly, advertising can be a powerful tool in a takeover battle. Advertising can accomplish several things effectively. For example, it can reach shareholders who hold stock in street name, as well as large numbers of employees and their families scattered around the country. Advertising can reach into another company's backyard with an impact that no other medium can match.

Ads also offer the opportunity for last-minute messages when there's no time to develop a full public relations campaign, or in a proxy fight, when the vote is close and one side or the other wishes to reach shareholders for a final push.

COMMUNICATIONS' STRATEGY ROLE

If it sounds like much of the communicator's activity in a contested takeover involves getting out the news and responding in a timely, credible way to requests from the news media, security analysts, and arbitrageurs, that is true. But IR/public relations also has a crucial role in developing and carrying out strategy. And it is here that its participation can spell the difference between victory and defeat.

Effective takeover strategy springs from the experience and creativity of the players who are involved. Here are some of the kinds of strategic ideas that can be marshalled, and some examples of contests in which they proved effective.

• *Mobilizing Constituents.* While there is less opportunity to use this technique today than in recent years, one effective approach has been to mobilize a company's employees and plant communities against an offer that would potentially result in closed or scaled-down facilities, lost jobs, and an economic blow to the community.

In the Marathon-Mobil contest cited at the beginning of this chapter, Marathon employees and citizens of Marathon's headquarters community, Findlay, Ohio, demonstrated fiercely against a takeover by Mobil. The newspapers and the major television networks covered the demonstrations. Commentators credit the demonstrations and the coverage they generated with helping create the political and judicial climate that enabled Marathon to prevail.

• *Challenge whether the raider is acting in the public interest.* Mobil was vulnerable in its Marathon bid to questions about whether it was behaving as Mobil itself said an oil company should behave.

Marathon drafted a short statement asking whether an oil company should be spending money on an acquisition when it should be searching for oil. Marathon Mailgrammed the statement to editorial writers for every paper in the United States. It also broadcast the statement by satellite. Editorial writers picked up on the issue that Mobil wanted to spend money on an acquisition during an oil shortage. Television stations around the country aired the satellite-transmitted statement.

Marathon also researched Mobil's public affairs ads on the Op-Ed page of the *New York Times*. It asked how Mobil's offer squared with its avowed commitment to finding oil to relieve the U.S. dependence on foreign petroleum. One ad said,

We ask Mobil: How is the national interest served by your proposed takeover of Marathon?

• *Damaging the raider's financing.* A critical factor for a hostile bidder is having the financing to pursue its offer. If a target company can come up with a way to shake that financing, it can often deal the bidder a mortal blow.

In Mesa's bid for Unocal, the target company was able to capitalize on the existing public climate concerning takeovers by publicly questioning the whole concept of federally chartered banks' lending money for takeovers. Unocal pressured Security Pacific, Mesa's principal bank, into quitting its banking relationship with Mesa.

Unocal filed a lawsuit against Security Pacific charging that it had breached fiduciary responsibility by lending to Mesa and misused confidential information about Unocal. Unocal also mailed copies of this lawsuit to other banks lending to Mesa. This letter implied that they might be next; the result was that one of Unocal's consortium of banks withdrew, forcing it to find other means of financing the takeover.

• *Prompting key constituent defections.* Learning that one of a company's key constituent groups will defect if a hostile offer is pursued — and publicizing that knowledge — can provide a "show-stopper" in a takeover fight.

When Western Pacific bought a block of Houghton Mifflin stock, several Houghton Mifflin authors, who accounted for more than half of the company's revenues, wrote to Mickey Newman, the CEO at Western Pacific, and told him they would not work for a conglomerate. If he proceeded with what looked like a takeover attempt, they said they would contract with another publisher.

Houghton Mifflin provided the *Boston Globe* with copies of the authors' letters, generating an in-depth story that included interviews with some of the authors. Newman eventually withdrew his overtures toward Houghton Mifflin.

NEW RULES OF THE GAME

As this chapter was readied for publication, important legal developments affecting takeovers were pending.

The U.S. Supreme Court upheld an Indiana law that gave strong ammunition to a company under attack — allowing it to call a meeting after a 50-day delay in which shareholders would decide whether the acquisitor of a large block would be able to vote his shares. Other states were moving to adopt similar legislation.

At the same time, Congress was holding hearings on the takeover phenomenon, with a view to enacting legislation to curtail insider trading and other perceived abuses in takeovers.

But it appears that as long as there are acquisitive instincts and prospect of enhanced values, corporate takeovers will continue. And because the effective dissemination of information is such a major consideration in contests for control, it seems certain that communications will have a key role in whatever shape the takeover game of the future assumes.

* * * * *

Richard E. Cheney is chairman of Hill and Knowlton and one of the nation's most experienced advisors on proxy contests and takeovers.

Edward O. Raynolds is senior vice president of Hill and Knowlton and deputy manager of its financial relations division.

CORPORATE INVESTOR RELATIONS IN MERGERS AND ACQUISITIONS

Robert W. Taft and Carol J. Makovich
Hill and Knowlton, Inc.

The number of corporate mergers and acquisitions climbs each year. Behind the activity, an intense policy debate continues: It is difficult to make the case that mergers and acquisitions are beneficial and increasing evidence suggests that most mergers don't work out. Further, the underlying reasons for merger and acquisition activity have changed. Until quite recently, most mergers occurred because buyer or seller believed that the business in question would do better under new ownership and new management. Today, a merger or acquisition may be triggered by a real or anticipated takeover threat.

This trend has affected the role of communications as well. In the past, communications strategies addressed the fundamentals and health of the underlying business and the question of how one business "fit" with the other. As hostile takeovers become increasingly common, communications is playing an important role in explaining and "selling" merger transactions to investors, employees, and other corporate audiences.

In most cases, takeovers require significant changes in a company's structure, goals, and business practices. A board of directors must define a valid business purpose for its moves in order to fulfill its fiduciary obligations. All this activity spells fundamental communications problems for the seller, the buyer,

195

and the operation that is bought or sold. All three change in important ways; the credible explanation of that change is an essential part of the success of the transaction.

OVERVIEW

In merger/acquisition situations, there are six principal areas of "relations." Each plays a vital role in making a merger/acquisition work, and communications with these six groups require prior planning and teamwork, internally and with your public relations counsel. The six areas are:

- Investor relations
- Community relations
- Media relations
- Employee communications
- Customer relations
- Shareholder relations

Good ongoing relations with these audiences is crucial during a takeover. The IR manager should coordinate his activities with other communications areas. He not only has a role to play in each situation, but he must also help assure that the company speaks with one voice to all important audiences.

As far as his own role is concerned, the IR manager can do several things to prepare for a merger/acquisition. The five guidelines we offer below will be useful in both friendly and unfriendly transactions:

- Do your job well in the first place.
- Know your management and your company.
- Plan for the unexpected.
- Know the rules regarding disclosure.
- Anticipate questions.

We will also suggest specific advice to help the IR manager with the four possible merger/acquisition scenarios:

- An uncontested "friendly" transaction with your company taking the lead.

- A friendly situation with your company merged into or acquired by another company.
- A contested (hostile) takeover with your company as an aggressor.
- A hostile situation with your company as a target.

Do Your Job Well in the First Place

There is a direct relationship between ongoing financial communications and the success or failure of communications for a merger/acquisition, friendly or unfriendly. Your company's previous record in corporate communications determines how a merger/acquisition is perceived and accepted by the financial community. If your management establishes a consistent, credible relationship with security analysts, shareholders, and the business and financial media, merger/acquisition communications campaigns are far more likely to achieve goals. A management that ignores these important audiences until a raider appears is less likely to do a good job. The Street will not believe management has the ability to change. A takeover crisis, in particular, is no time to try to establish credibility. Of course, the best defense against a takeover is a fully valued share price. Investor relations managers who do their job right are already helping their companies discourage hostile takeover efforts.

KNOW YOUR MANAGEMENT AND YOUR COMPANY

Part of your planning will have to take into consideration your management's current relationship with the financial community. What's management's track record with acquisitions? If prior acquisitions haven't worked well, what's different about this transaction? Why should the financial community believe that it will work better than the others? If the transaction represents the first time your company has expanded through merger/acquisition, how can you establish management's ability to successfully integrate and run a new operation? Be aware of any skeletons in your corporate closet that might be dragged out during a contest, and be prepared to explain them quickly and directly. Your management should be briefed regarding the possibility of personal attacks.

Analyze your board of directors. What is their individual track record in supporting managements under siege? Would your management stand up under pressure? If your management is inexperienced in dealing with the media and the financial community while under fire, schedule confrontation training. Establish crisis clearance procedures in order to facilitate issuance of statements and releases. Make sure everyone knows what priorities are in a crisis.

Know your market and your shareholders. Many companies find that the most useful function of a stock-watch service is the familiarity they develop with stock trading patterns. This kind of familiarity, combined with regular analysis and identification of shareholders, increases your ability to spot unusual trading patterns and to know when it's time to sound the alarm. Track major shareholders, and make sure you know who the appropriate decision-maker is at each institution with substantial shareholdings.

Plan for the Unexpected

Sometimes an IR manager has ample time to plan merge/acquisition communications. Sometimes not. However, good public relations practice includes planning for the unexpected. One obvious point that deserves emphasis is that good media and analyst relations are essential during a takeover.

Much can be done in advance to prepare for quick, effective response to a hostile takeover or to position a sudden acquisition decision. Keep your list of contacts and other related information current. This includes home telephone numbers of key management and executives at your company, as well as your outside public relations counsel, proxy solicitation and investment banking people, and legal counsel. Add numbers for key media, as well as media deadlines for news announcements and ad placements. Include locations and contacts for press conference and teleconference facilities. Make sure media and analyst lists are kept up-to-date as well. You may need them in a hurry, especially during a takeover fight. Keep a separate list of analysts, reporters, and editors who are friendly and knowledgeable about the company. If you have ignored the press in the past, don't expect them to return your calls when you need them to explain a transaction during a takeover.

Know the Rules Regarding Disclosure

The IR manager and corporate counsel are responsible for advising management regarding required disclosure for a merger/ acquisition. In the best of all worlds, the IR manager will know early on if top management is involved in merger/acquisition talks and can brief management on disclosure obligations.

If your top management is secretive and inclined to call in the communications staff at the last minute, take the initiative and brief management on the special problems associated with merger/acquisition negotiations disclosure before the fact.

To be fully prepared for any and all possible releases during a merger/acquisition, consider drafting the following:

- Stand-by release in case of unexpected activity in the stock.
- Response to inquiries about market reaction, e.g., NYSE inquires about possible merger/acquisition discussions.
- Announcement of intent.
- Confirmation of negotiations.
- Announcement of merger/acquisition discussions, naming parties.
- Preliminary agreement (joint announcement).
- Agreement in principle (joint announcement).
- Agreement to purchase.
- Definitive agreement and outline of merger/acquisition process (joint announcement).
- Shareholder approval.
- Completion of merger/acquisition.

If not doing so already, the IR professional should keep a close watch on stock activity as soon as he is aware of the merger/acquisition talks. If the stock begins to show unusual activity, the IR person can then discuss the disclosure issues with management. If merger/acquisition confidentiality is strictly maintained and no rumors circulate, there is no legal requirement for a public announcement while negotiations are in progress.

SEC regulations don't compel a company to comment about merger discussions. However, if a company comments in response to stock exchange or regulatory inquiry, it must do so truthfully, and must acknowledge that merger discussions are taking place. It must also update its comments on the discussions. Since most companies prefer to negotiate privately, there are very few examples of disclosures while merger discussions are in progress.

The "No Comment" Solution

In 1984, the courts began to consider when communications about mergers might be misleading. The first important case involved Heublein defending itself against a takeover threat by merging with R.J.R. Nabisco. Heublein issued statements saying it knew of no reason for trading in its stock. At the time of the statements, Heublein was talking merger with Nabisco. The court held that the statements were not misleading.

The next year the court looked at a case involving Carnation. Although the facts were slightly different, Carnation issued the then standard comment that it knew of no reason for activity in its stock at a time when it was secretly engaged in merger discussions with Nestle. The court said Carnation's statements were misleading and rejected the Heublein case.

Since Carnation, the best legal advice has been to say "No comment." Say "No comment" to the stock exchange when the department of stock list calls. Say "No comment" even if the stock exchange threatens to delist you. Say "No comment" even though the phrase has become a buzzword that the Street understands probably means that something is going on.

Several jurisdictions are following the Carnation decision, but other courts prefer the Heublein logic. The Supreme Court is about to consider the question, and we recommend you review your comments with counsel before saying anything in this area, since the rules are changing.

Anticipate Questions

In any acquisition situation, numerous questions from all audiences are bound to occur, ranging from basic operational questions from employees to highly technical questions from security analysts. We advise clients to take control of the situation by releasing as much information as possible as early as possible. It is advisable to develop a Q & A book about the merger/acquisition as a standard reference for all inquiries. Portions of the book may be reproduced for distribution to all important corporate audiences. Once the Q & A book and other materials are ready, you will be prepared for an onslaught of calls. Available spokespeople for the media, in particular, should be clearly defined and limited to one — at most two. If two, they should confer frequently. All employees should be alerted to the names of contacts as well as their phone numbers.

What the Financial Community Wants to Know

The IR manager's key focus is to anticipate the financial community's questions about the merger/acquisition and to address those concerns.

Analysts will want answers to questions such as: Why did ABC Corporation decide to buy XYZ, Inc.? What's the timetable and plan for merging operations, or will the acquired entity continue to operate as a subsidiary? Will the transaction result in a major restructuring of the combined company? What cost efficiencies will be accomplished, and how? Which operations or facilities will be closed or combined? What are the labor implications of the combination? What are the compensation and pension implications of the transaction? What's the effect on customers and customer service? Will key management members of the acquired company stay or go? Will the new entity do business under a new name? What is the new stock symbol? Where will shares be traded?

If the acquired entity will require substantial investment from its new parent as well as significant management time, address these issues in-depth. Security analysts and professional money managers will want to know the particulars regarding the investment of money and labor.

The same logic outlined for security analysts applies for institutional investors. Compare your company's investment profile before and after the merger/acquisition. What's the effect on your PE, shares outstanding, market capitalization, and debt ratios? What's the net effect on your balance sheet and outlook? Is the company buying a thriving operation, or purchasing a soso performer with potential that thrusts management into a turnaround situation? Will the operations be merged or continue to operate as separate units?

Communicating to Employees about Their Pensions and Benefits

The first question any employee asks is, "Do I still have a job?" The second question is, "What about my pension?" To protect executive pensions, a few companies are beginning to create special funds that shelter pension funds should a takeover or merger occur. The safest of these trusts are those that offer immediate vesting of executive pensions, as the so-called secular trusts do. Since these financing options are complicated, they should be investigated and established before a crisis occurs.

Normally an IR manager does not become involved in communications with employees about their pensions. However, there are two reasons we believe it is an appropriate topic for IR in a merger situation. First, analysts normally seek information on how excess pension benefits will be used in the new entity; and second, changes in the pension funding are often an important reason for the transaction.

UNCONTESTED MERGERS/ACQUISITIONS

Your first task as an IR practitioner in a friendly merger/ acquisition in which your company is the leader in the transaction is to develop a position statement regarding the merger/ acquisition. Corporate position statements, when well-written and carefully implemented, set the stage for broad understanding of a merger, acquisition, or divestiture. This statement should include key messages to be emphasized about the transaction, particularly the fit with current corporate strategy, synergism with existing operations or added value brought to the new operation from the acquirer, and the benefits to shareholders. The statement should also include enough human values to provide a degree of comfort to employees facing the uncertainty of whether they will have jobs and who their new boss may be. For example, prudent raiders generally acknowledge with respect the reputation of the companies they seek to acquire.

POSITIONING

As soon an agreement in principle has been reached, the top priority is to execute communications to position the merger/acquisition favorably. Your premerger and postmerger communications will be most effective if you identify the positive and negative aspects of the transaction and produce communications that emphasize the positives while directly addressing the negatives.

A merger/acquisition can be friendly on both sides, yet can be controversial for shareholders. Shareholders of both companies involved should be informed about the merger/acquisition through a letter from their respective chairs. This letter should outline the terms of the merger/acquisition agreement and its anticipated fit into the company's future.

If the merger/acquisition requires shareholder support, ask the proxy solicitor to perform a premeeting vote analysis. Most solicitors can review your shareholder list and predict a likely outcome for the vote. If the outcome is in doubt, work with your solicitor to mail special letters to shareholders — one that precedes the proxy statement and one that accompanies it. Large holders should be visited personally by a member of top management. At these meetings, shareholders will voice their objections, and management has a chance to address holders directly and convince them of the wisdom of the transaction.

On the day the merger/acquisition is announced, information packages on both companies should be distributed to analysts following the companies. To prepare for press inquiries, inhouse corporate contacts at both companies should be thoroughly briefed and armed with the position statement and Q & A book.

When news of a merger/acquisition first hits, it is important to have the analysts' full understanding and "approval" of the transaction. Business and financial reporters increasingly contact analysts for their assessment and analysis of a merger/acquisition situation. You may want to give the press a list of analysts who are particularly close to your company and your merger/acquisition partner. The list will help reporters by saving their time and energies, and afford you a level of control over who they contact for comment.

Once the merger/acquisition is complete, schedule a meeting or series of meetings with analysts during the first quarter following consummation of the transaction.

Postmerger/Acquisition Considerations

The task of effectively communicating about a merger/acquisition continues long after the initial activities described so far. The IR manager must continue to keep the financial community up-to-date on the progress of consolidation and strides made by the new entity. Such news can be highlighted in press releases or given attention in quarterly reports. The annual report is an excellent vehicle to highlight positive progress after a merger/acquisition. Also, when planning post–merger/acquisition analyst presentations, invite members of the new management team to address the analysts about their portion of the combined operations.

If the acquired entity is in a similar line of business, it's likely that your analyst following will either remain the same or expand to include analysts who follow the acquired company.

However, if the merger/acquisition involves a brand-new business for your company, postmerger communications must recognize that security analysts will need to be educated regarding the diversification strategy and the new business your company has acquired. Your company's new configuration might encourage other security analysts — such as diversified company analysts or special situations analysts — to begin coverage. Whatever the case, assess how the merger/acquisition will impact the analysts' incentive to follow your company and plan accordingly.

RESEARCH

In our experience, little or no research is done at the time of a merger/acquisition. This is regrettable, and we continue to urge that fundamental attitudinal research be conducted to gain a better understanding of the reactions of all parties affected by the transaction and critical to the merger's future success.

The opinions of the financial community are the most visible and least in need of research. Market price will quickly tell you whether the Street believes the merger will work, whether it believes the price was fair, and whether the transaction solves or creates problems. Newspaper accounts suggest the merger of Sperry and Burrows (now Unisys) was "tested" on the Street in a series of rumors and premerger leaks before the companies were willing to proceed.

The attitudes of employees and shareholders are far less visible but just as important. The purpose of the research is not to determine "what they think" of the deal, for the transaction is a given. Rather the research identifies basic problems that an integrative communications effort must seek to address. Once these problems are identified, the IR manager should work with other relations professionals to develop an action plan.

When Your Company is Acquired

The first question that occurs to managers in this situation is, "Will I keep my job?" Maybe. Maybe not. If the combined entity is large enough, it's possible that a new IR department can accommodate both existing IR staffs. Whatever the ultimate outcome — and you may not know that for some months — the best course of action is to cooperate fully with the staff of the acquiring company. Become a visible part of the merger/acquisition team managing all the activities we've just described. Be open, creative, helpful. You could increase your chances to join the reorganized IR department. If you must leave, take advantage of these new contacts to help find another position.

CONTESTED MERGERS/ACQUISITIONS

Leading the Charge

Most frequently, the IR manager at a company contemplating an unfriendly takeover has a key advantage over his counterpart at the target: time. Use this advantage well. While the lawyers and proxy solicitors are fighting it out in the courts and on the telephone, your role is to help manage the communications aspects of the fight: the press, letters to shareholders, materials for security analysts and institutional shareholders, and public statements. Your analysis and counsel should focus on two groups: your own company's financial audience and that of the target.

As with a friendly merger/acquisition, you will have to successfully "sell" the benefits of the transaction to your own security analysts, institutional and individual shareholders, and financial media contacts. As soon as the takeover is out in the open, make sure all these parties hear from you. Spell out the reasons that make the takeover advantageous and seek support for the transaction. You don't want to see an analyst who knows your company well saying in the press that the takeover is a bad idea.

As we mentioned before, anticipate the questions and concerns and be ready to address them. Will the analysts — both your company's and the target's — think you're paying too much for the target? Will the analysts agree that management time and company funds are well-spent pursuing an expensive takeover battle? Is this the first time your management has undertaken a hostile takeover? Or is this one of a series of hostile takeovers, and if so, what kind of track record has your management established?

Monitoring the press is crucial during a takeover attempt.

Find out what's being said and identify what requires a response and what can be used to your advantage. Look for opportunities for broad visibility of your management's message, in both print and broadcast media. Use your lead time to identify key analysts and reporters who cover the target. Be prepared to answer charges and arguments that are bound to appear in the press from the target management.

Outside public relations counsel can be particularly valuable in assisting you with the broad press relations and monitoring required during a fight, as well as in providing additional "arms and legs" to cope with the massive volume of communications during the fight.

We mentioned early on that IR is only one part of total communications during a merger/acquisitions. The IR manager should be mindful that messages directed to investors during a fight will also reach the other three important audiences: employees, communities, and customers of both your company and the target. The target's employees and communities have played pivotal roles in the outcome of a number of contested takeovers. Assess the impact of your messages on these groups and direct special messages to them, if appropriate.

IR for a Takeover Defense

Our colleagues Cheney and Raynolds have addressed hostile takeovers in another section of this book, so our discussion of takeover defenses will be brief. Companies have developed several effective strategies for thwarting a hostile takeover. More and more managements are restructuring their own operations on the theory that they'd rather do it to themselves than have a raider do it. Many companies are undervalued and are especially vulnerable to takeover. A restructuring or a recapitalization to reallocate and increase management's percentage of ownership tends to discourage a hostile bid by reducing or eliminating the undervaluation. In most recapitalization the market value of the recapitalized company may rise dramatically, making it more costly to acquire the company. In addition, the recapitalization may result in disposition of certain divisions or assets that a bidder might consider particularly desirable.

Standard & Poor's *Credit Review* annually reports a summary of changes in corporate credit ratings. One of its conclusions is that while major acquirers or other companies involved in restructurings frequently suffer downgradings in the ratings of their debt securities, target companies that still have debt outstanding after a deal often enjoy a rise in ratings. The report concludes, however, that recapitalizations under the threat of a hostile takeover are the most damaging to credit quality.

Although recapitalization may ward off a hostile suitor, it poses serious ramifications for the threatened company. And, despite defensive measures, many hostile takeover attempts are successful. Several factors have contributed to an environment that encourages hostile takeovers.

Shareholder Loyalty

Most public relations texts discuss shareholder communications in terms of developing "shareholder loyalty." It is time to acknowledge that shareholders have become more sophisticated and that shareholder loyalty is, if not a thing of the past, at least seriously eroded.

For one thing, corporate raiders have become respectable. Not only do respected companies now make raids, but some individual raiders are business "celebrities" prominently featured on bookshelves, on talk shows, and testifying in the halls of Congress.

Also institutional ownership has led to an increased emphasis by the "owners" on short-term profit objectives. At this writing, the institutions are engaged in a systematic challenge to "poison pills" (which were adopted by boards without the requirement of shareholder approval) for the simple reason that a poison pill makes it somewhat more difficult for a raider to acquire a company (and reward the shareholder with short-term profit).

The Company as Poker Chip

Today's business media reflect and enhance a spirit of "gamesmanship" that infects Wall Street, the business schools, and, increasingly, the managements of major companies. But for every raider playing the game there are thousands of pawns who do not control the play and who are, in a sense, its victims.

Certain company divisions are sold and sold again, often four or more times in the course of a few years. In this environment it is difficult to communicate corporate information and nearly impossible to effectively articulate corporate objectives that will inspire and motivate employees and shareholders. It is possible to staff and operate a business with employees who do not feel traditional corporate loyalty, but it is essential that a company understand why its employees stay in their jobs and what motivates them to do well.

The idea of "break-up value" is widely understood and widely written about. Research houses specialize in a form of securities analysis that defines the worth of each piece of a business were it to be sold. Most employees know or can easily learn what offers can be made that will oblige management to consider disposing of the operating unit and possibly their job.

Most alert managers are also aware that they may be able to make a bid, in the form of a leveraged buyout (LBO), for their piece of the company or (if they are senior enough) for the whole company. They tend to know where the fat is and have given thought to how they would operate the company differently should it become necessary to run the business to.generate cash to pay down the debt created in the LBO.

Rites and Rituals

So far, few corporations are doing a very good job of communicating about mergers and acquisitions. A recent study suggests that about 80 percent of all U.S. corporate name changes in 1986 were the result of a merger, acquisition, or restructuring. The same study suggested that a name change occurs in about 25 percent of the mergers and acquisitions that occur. In this environment, the company becomes a business opportunity with a specific current value. The abstractions that fueled loyalty to growing enterprises in the past tend to be irrelevant today.

By definition, a merger or acquisition mandates a change in corporate culture of both the acquirer and the acquiree. In *Corporate Culture,* Terrence Deal and Allan Kennedy articulated a number of abstractions that most people familiar with a corporate environment had intuitively understood existed but had failed to describe so well. The authors discuss the problems of "managing the change" at some length and offer these tips:

- Recognize that peer group consensus will be the major influence on acceptance or willingness to change.
- Convey and emphasize two-way trust in all matters (and especially communications) related to change.
- Think of change as skill building and concentrate on training as part of the change process.
- Allow enough time for change to take hold.
- Encourage people to adapt the basic idea for the change to fit the real world around them.

It is beyond the scope of this chapter to discuss the role of corporate culture in detail. But the final words of *Corporate Culture* are relevant:

> In sum, the future holds promise for strong culture companies. Strong cultures are not only able to respond to an environment, but they also adapt to diverse and changing circumstances. When times are tough, these companies can reach deeply into their shared values and beliefs for the truth and courage to see them through. When new challenges arise, they can adjust. This is exactly what companies are going to have to do as we begin to experience a revolution in the structure of modern organizations.

* * * * *

Robert W. Taft is senior vice president of Hill and Knowlton and an author-attorney who writes and consults about complex issues of corporate financings, investment transactions, and litigation.

Carol J. Makovich is senior vice president in Hill and Knowlton's financial relations division.

RAISING THE INFORMATION CONTENT OF THE MD&A

LeRoy A. Glasner, Jr., CFA
The Financial Relations Board, Inc.

The published testimony of investment professionals establishes that the annual report, and especially its management discussion and analysis section (MD&A), is a primary source of information and interpretation used in their deliberations. Logic suggests that the MD&A be a readable and read section of the annual, organized to convey clearly the investment story and to present meaningfully the implication of the financial past with respect to the future.

One corporate attitude holds that it is not the responsibility of the corporation to do the analyst's homework. This attitude, sometimes tied to a fear of competitors knowing too much, causes the corporation to report the barest minimum required by the SEC.

Other managements recognize that their securities are in competition with other stocks, bonds, coins, antiques, and the entire spectrum of investment possibilities. They enhance their competitive position in the capital market by making useful information available and accessible to the investment community.

By doing so, the investment risk is reduced (in "present value" analysis, the discount rate drops), making analysis easier and forecasts more certain for those who put their reputations on the line when they recommend or buy specific securities.

Furthermore, there is a new and rapidly growing number of money managers with assets of $25 million to $100 million. There also is a growing stable of independent portfolio managers within large institutions who do their own homework and make their own decisions. They rely on the MD&A for financial data supplied in accessible form to reduce the time required to reach a decision.

As a further and perhaps more compelling inducement, the SEC's enforcement attitude may have stiffened with respect to the MD&A. The Director of the Division of Corporate Finance of the SEC has said that the staff will issue fewer comment letters on filed documents suggesting changes in future filings, and will instead focus on matters that require the amendment of documents on file. The Director has also said the SEC will continue to refer to the MD&A as a starting point for enforcement actions, and continues to believe that management has a positive duty to disclose both positive and negative information in the MD&A.

The following pages are a compendium of ideas and techniques aimed at expanding the information content of the MD&A, reducing the risk of owning the company's securities, and thereby reducing the cost of capital.

THE TYPICAL MD&A

Most public companies offer a "discussion" that is not "analysis," but that generally satisfies the minimum regulatory requirements. The typical offering ignores the most significant mandates of Regulations S-K and S-X: "enhance reader's understanding," "relevant trends," "assess amounts and certainty of cash flow," "past events and uncertainties not representative," "in relation to whole business," and "presently known data which will impact results." However, the SEC has not widely challenged that prevailing practice. The consequence of this corporate attitude and slack enforcement often is a bland, trivial recitation of a few facts and figures already given elsewhere in the annual report, accompanied by innocuous text.

BASIC MD&A DISCLOSURE REQUIREMENTS

As background, it is helpful to review the minimum MD&A disclosure requirements promulgated by the SEC under the Securities Act of 1934, contained in Regulations S-K and S-X and specifically prescribed in the Guide to the Preparation of Form 10-K. A summary of the pertinent rules and the accompanying instructions follows:

(S-K Item 303): Rules and Instructions

Rules

Full Fiscal Years. Discuss financial condition, changes in financial condition, and results of operations, including comment on liquidity and capital resources — discussions that may be combined if interrelated. Where a discussion of segments or other subdivision is judged appropriate, focus on each relevant section and on registrant as a whole.

Liquidity. Identify known long-term and short-term factors or uncertainties that could or will cause a material change in liquidity. Indicate the course of action to resolve a deficiency. Identify and describe internal and external sources. Discuss material unused sources.

Capital Resources. Describe capital expenditure commitments as to amount, purpose, and source of funds. Describe favorable and unfavorable trends, indicate expected material changes in mix and relative cost, and discuss changes in debt-equity ratio and off-balance sheet financing.

Results of Operations. Describe unusual events or economic changes materially affecting income from continuing operations, and, *in each case,* indicate extent of impact. Describe known trends or uncertainties that could or will have a material impact on sales or income from continuing operations. Discuss material sales increases in terms of volume, price, and new product or service effects. Discuss impact of inflation on sales/revenues and income from operations.

Instructions

1. Discussion and analysis should be of statements and data presented to enhance reader's understanding of financial condition, changes therein, and results of operations. Generally, data shall discuss "three year period" and shall use year-to-year comparisons or other formats. Where trends are relevant, reference to five-year data may be necessary.

2. Purpose is to give information to help users assess the amounts and certainty of cash flow from operations and from outside sources.

3. Focus specifically on material events and uncertainties that could cause the past to be unrepresentative of the future.

4. Causes of material changes in the line items should be described in relation to whole business. Need not recite amount of changes readily computable. Discussion should not merely repeat data from the statements.

5. "Liquidity" refers to the ability to generate adequate amounts of cash. Company should indicate how its liquidity should be measured and discuss those indicators on a short-term and long-term basis.

6. Discuss restrictions on transfer of funds between registrant and subsidiaries.

7. Forward-looking information is encouraged, not required, but is distinguished from presently known data that will impact results. For example, known increases in labor and raw material costs "may be required to be disclosed." "Safe harbor" rule would apply to projections.

8. Where required, FAS 33 narrative description and data may be combined with discussion prescribed by this item.

9. Where FAS 33 data are not required, discuss inflation in whatever manner appears appropriate.

BASIC MD&A SUBJECT MATTER AND TASK

It is likewise helpful to recall that FAS 1 says the primary purpose of financial reporting is to furnish information to investors with which they can forecast future cash flow available to finance the business and pay dividends. In other words, *the business process is the basic subject matter of financial accounting,* and the task of financial accounting is to describe how the process works to generate returns to investors. The data and text of the MD&A should be organized and presented with reference to the business process, as it occurs, from the investors' point of view.

BUSINESS PROCESS FROM THE INVESTOR'S VIEWPOINT

The annual business process is presented graphically in Exhibit 1. It begins with (1) an investment by shareholders, which is leveraged (2) through liabilities to suppliers, including employees, banks, and other creditors. The total funds are used (3) to acquire assets to manufacture a product or render a service that is (4) offered for sale. Expenses attributable to (5) and taxes chargeable against the sales generated (6) are deducted to

EXHIBIT 1

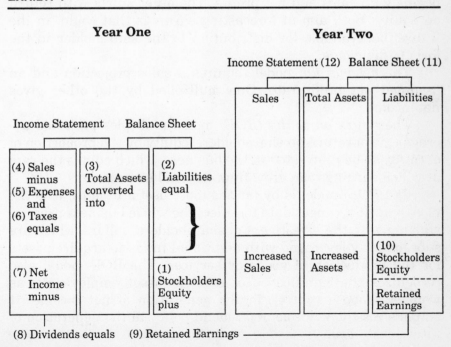

arrive at (7) net income, from which (8) a dividend may be deducted. The balance constitutes (9) retained earnings, an expansion of (10) the equity base, which increment may be leveraged to initiate the next phase of growth, based on (11) an expanded balance sheet with the potential of (12) increased sales and net income.

ORGANIZING DATA TO DESCRIBE THE BUSINESS PROCESS

The instructions to S-K Item 303 deserve very careful consideration because they collectively convey the intent of the rules. That intent is central to our conviction that any meaningful discussion must be conducted in reference to some organizing principle, aimed at establishing by implication (at worst), or specific statement (at best), the future financial prospects of the reporting company as they may affect security holders.

A survey of several hundred research directors shows that there are two basic organizing methods in general use. One begins with sales and net profits. The other starts with return on equity. Both aim at forecasting earnings that could, in the future, be available for distribution to the shareholder in the form of dividends.

The *net margin* model requires a sales projection and an assumed net profit rate. One multiplied by the other gives net income.

The *return on equity (ROE)* model multiples projected average rate of return on shareholders' equity by the proportion of earnings to be reinvested in the business, which equals the rate at which earnings can grow from internal sources.

The *ROE* model is by far the most useful because it is the most *real*. It arranges data to reflect the whole business process, starting with the investment of shareholders' dollars, which are subsequently leveraged with additional funds to acquire assets for the production of goods or services. The ROE model also recognizes the significance of efficient asset employment, as well as expense control, in the generation of net income. It emphasizes the key role of dividend policy in the generation of future cash flow.

The ROE model and versions of it are known by various names: *implied growth, sustainable growth, strategic profit, earning power* — to name a few. By whatever name, it is an organizational framework that makes sense of the mountain of data confronting the investor, simplifying the analytical task and reducing the time required to make a decision.

Essentially, the ROE model projects the level of sales, assets, and stockholders' equity supported by and resulting from reinvested earnings and then assumes a rate of return to be earned on these earnings sources. Since rates of return can only be so high, sales, assets and equity are the long-term determinants of growth.

Focusing attention on the long-term growth determinants puts the short-term fluctuations in rates of return into appropriate perspective, turning attention from interim deviations in a company's operating record to the long-term potential for expansion through retained earnings or the sale of new shares. The model is therefore an ideal device to use in developing a meaningful MD&A.

THE ROE MODEL

The basic ROE model is:

Return on equity		Retention rate		Sustainable growth rate	
ROE	x	RR	=	SGR	(A)

Amplification of that equation has taken several forms and been carried to great lengths. The following amplification, employing beginning equity and assets, is presented as a useful starting point:

Net margin		Beginning asset turnover		Return on beginning assets		Beginning financial leverage		Return on beginning equity	
NM	x	T/O	=	ROBA	x	LEV	=	ROBE	(B)

Return on equity		Retention rate		Sustainable growth rate	
ROE	x	RR	=	SGR	(C)

Beginning Versus Ending or Average Equity

There is no *a priori* "correct" value for assets or equity in the ROE model. The "best" value is the one that's the easiest to use for the purpose of projecting future earnings. It is easier, in our judgment, to work with beginning assets and equity, since fewer quantities must be forecast to develop a hypothesis about the earnings potential for the period ahead.

For example, if beginning equity is 10% greater on January 1, 1988, than on January 1, 1987, and the rate of return is unchanged, net income will be up 10%. One need only project the rate of return.

If average or ending equity is used, either must first be projected — and the amounts projected are dependent on the rate of return earned during the year and the proportion of earnings retained. One must project at least two dependent variables. So for the purpose of investment analysis, beginning values are favored for convenience.

Adapting the Model for the MD&A.

As the basic model illustrates, long-term internal growth derives from earnings retained and reinvested in the business.

The amplified model implies that the growth is realized if the increased equity base is leveraged to acquire additional assets, and those assets in turn generate sales. Therefore, sales and assets, as well as equity, are growth sources, and collectively comprise a company's *earnings base.*

The *earning power* of the earnings base is a function of the expected rates of return on the constituent parts. Exhibit 2 illustrates how the concepts of earnings base and rates of return can be combined to develop an estimate of earning power.

Company A, currently registering a loss of $2.50 a share, could have an earning power of $4.50 a share, based on the historic average rates of return. Company B, with earnings of $2.50, could have an earning power of $1.25 based on historic average rates, and $4.50 based on a new management's restructuring strategy and future rate of return goals.

In brief, the past can be explained by describing and accounting for expansion of the earnings base and changes in the

EXHIBIT 2

Company	Rate of Return	Sales $100	Assets $50	Equity $25	EPS Earning Power
		Earnings Base Constituents			
A	Current	–2.5%	–5.0%	–10.0%	$(2.50)
	Historic	5.0%	10.0%	20.0%	$4.50
B	Current	2.5%	5.0%	10.0%	$2.50
	Historic	1.25%	2.5%	5.0%	$1.25
	Future	5.0%	10.0%	20.0%	$4.50

rates of return. Future potential can be assessed by (1) determining current earning power and (2) factoring in the sustainable growth rate. By that means, the ROE model can be adapted to use in the MD&A.

THE MODIFIED ROE MODEL

If the ROE/Sustainable Growth Model is judged inappropriate, an ROE-only version is a worthwhile alternate means of organizing financial data and discussion. Simply confine the discussion to formula (B):

$$NM \times T/O = ROBA \times LEV = ROBE$$

Although less comprehensive than the expanded model, the ROE-only version does highlight key measures of management operating efficiency and financial policy. Exhibit 3 is useful in focusing the discussion.

EXHIBIT 3

	5-Year Average	Last Year	Future Goals
Net Margin x	1.25%	3.00%	5.0%
Asset Turnover =	2.0x	2.5x	3.0x
ROBA x	2.5%	7.5%	15%
Leverage =	2.0x	2.0x	1.5x
ROBE	5.0%	15.0%	27.5%

FINANCIAL REVIEW TABLE OF CONTENTS

A roadmap to the financial review section encourages readability and reduces the time required to find the information sought. A simple listing of the required statements, with notes, is not adequate. Further detail is appropriate. For example:

Financial Review

Five-year operating and per share data.
Discussion of pertinent trends.
Past two years results of operation.
Earnings variance table.
Cash flow table.
Quarterly results and market information.
Segment and line of products data.
Industry information.

Financial Statements

Income and stockholder's equity.
Balance sheet.
Change in financial condition.

Financial Footnotes

Accounting principles.
Inventories.
Property, plant, and equipment.
Investments.
Long-term debt.
Earnings per share.

A RECAP OF PAST TRENDS

Regulatory intent aside, it is in the best interests of current or potential investors that the MD&A facilitate an efficient market for the company's securities. The typical MD&A is limited to a discussion of the two preceding 12-month periods, which could be misleadingly unrepresentative of the future. A recap of the past five 12-month periods is strongly recommended.

The earnings power/sustainable growth approach is illustrated below through analysis of the record of a highly leveraged startup.

Some modification of the sample language would be required in the case of a turnaround, a stable growth stock, or some permutation of those generic company circumstances. However, the basic expository approach is universally applicable.

Financial Recap Example

The financial record reflects earnings per share growth from 8¢ in 1982 to $1.45 for 1987. That gain was the consequence of:

- Vigorous expansion of the earnings base and
- rising rates of return on sales and assets,
- offset by a decrease in return on equity and
- increased number of shares outstanding.

Earnings Base

During the past five years, the three principal factors from which earnings are derived have increased at varying compound rates:

Stockholders' equity vaulted to $34.2 million from a modest $1.8 million. Assets reached $59.4 million compared with $18.4 million, while sales topped $152 million vs. $56 million, both rising at about 24% annually.

The marked difference in the growth of stockholder equity, in contrast to that of assets and sales, is a reflection of:

- The debt-heavy capital structure which followed the 1982 leveraged buyout of the company by present management from the prior corporate owner.
- Retention of all earnings to finance internal expansion.
- The sale of new shares to finance acquisitions.
- The success of the principal operation, which has progressed from marginal to substantial profitability.

In the future, the chief constituents of the earnings base should expand at about the same compound rate.

Suggested charts: Sales, assets, and equity for past six years with rates of change.

Rates of Return

The return on equity has dropped from unsustainable high, early levels as the retention of earnings and sale of shares to strengthen the balance sheet have reduced financial leverage from an excessive 13.3x to a conservative 1.9x. (See Selected Financial Data below.) Concurrently, return on beginning equity declined from 419% to 48% last year. In contrast, returns on assets and sales are substantially above the initial levels:

- 7.3% on sales, up from 0.9%.
- 26.2% on assets, up from 3.1%.

Those improvements resulted largely from enhanced operating profitability. On balance, asset turnover is about unchanged and the effective tax rate has been virtually constant. Therefore, the improved returns on assets and sales are traceable to the operating margin, which increased to 12.4% from 1.8%.

Selected Financial Data

Year	5	4	3	2	1
Financial leverage	1.9x	2.9x	5.4x	10.1x	13.3x
Asset turnover	3.6x	4.7x	4.6x	4.2x	3.5x
Tax rate	45%	46%	45%	44%	34%
Operating Margin	12.4%	10.8%	8.5%	6.9%	1.8%
Average shares (mil.)	7.7	7.1	6.5	6.4	6.1

Net Earnings and Earnings Per Share

Enhanced operating profitability caused net earnings to expand more rapidly than from the expanded earnings base alone. Thus, net earnings actually increased to $11.1 million from $0.5 million. And although year-end shares outstanding increased 26% to 7.7 million from 6.1 million, earnings per share nearly matched the net income record, rising to $1.45 from 8¢.

Suggested charts: Net earnings and earnings per share for past six years with rates of change, plus shares outstanding.

Sustainable Growth Rate

The company expects

- To achieve an average return on equity of 20% in the coming years, and
- To continue reinvesting all earnings.

In the short term, earnings variations may reflect changes in return on equity attributable to a variety of internal and/or external factors. As the cause of a short-term dislocation in the average rate of return dissipates or is corrected, earnings growth from internal funds will adjust to the company's sustainable internal-growth rate, determined by the normal rate of return and the dividend payout policy. Since the company retains 100% of earnings, the internal growth potential is equal to the projected average return on equity of 20%.

Suggested charts: Rates of return on sales, assets and equity for past five years.

NET INCOME VARIANCE TABLE OF LAST TWO YEARS

Most MD&A copy gets bogged down in a recitation of numbers and ratios, which can sorely try the patience of the most ardent cruncher of numbers. It's far better to begin with a table that shows all the relevant changes in one place. Exhibit 4 has proven useful:

The subsequent text can account for the changes observed giving further amplification. For example, instructions require

EXHIBIT 4 Net Income Variance (dollar figures in millions)

	Last Year vs. Prior Year				Prior Year vs. Year Before			
	$ Amt	%Sales	$Chng	%Chng	$Amt	%Sales	$Chng	%Chng
Net sales	18.0	100	2.8	18	15.3	100	2.0	15
Cost of sales	10.4	58	1.2	13	9.2	60	.6	7
Gross income	7.6	43	1.5	20	6.1	40	1.4	31
SG&A	4.4	24	.7	19	3.7	24	.6	18
Operating income	3.2	18	.8	33	2.4	16	.9	58
Net other incom & expense	.2	1	(.2)	(51)	.5	3	.1	43
Pretax income	3.1	17	1.1	57	1.9	13	.7	62
Provision for taxes	1.4	8	.8	120	.6	4	.2	35
Net income	1.7	9	.3	27	1.3	9	.6	79

that "material sales changes" be ascribed to "volume, price and new product" effects. That information could be given in the text, as could other data explaining changes.

EARNINGS PER SHARE VARIANCE

The change in earnings per share is the final focus of many investors. Several formats have been devised to account for the alteration in detail. Exhibit 5 incorporates two variance models:

EXHIBIT 5

	Year 1	Year 2
Changes in Earnings per Share		
Current year	$3.00	$2.00
Prior year	2.00	2.50
Net increase (decrease)	1.00	(0.50)
Variance Analysis by Income Source and Expense		
Net sales	$1.50	$.50
Volume	1.30	0.40
Selling prices	.20	.10
COS	(.65)	(.40)
SG&A	(.05)	(.10)
Depreciation	.10	(.50)
Currency fluctuation	.05	(.05)
Total operations	.95	(.70)
Interest expense	.05	.05
Corporate and other expenses	.05	.05
Shares outstanding	(.05)	.10
Net increase (decrease)	1.00	(0.50)
Variance Analysis by Source and Rate of Return		
Net margin	$.25	$(.65)
Asset turnover	.60	(.05)
Return on assets	.85	(.70)
Financial leverage	(.10)	.15
Return on equity	.75	(.60)
Equity per share	.30	—
Shares outstanding	(.05)	.10
Net increase (decrease)	1.00	(0.50)

(1) income source and expense, and (2) source and rate of return. Each can be used separately.

If space permits, the EPS variance tables are an ideal inclusion in the Shareholder Information page, which is recommended for every report (see "Segment Information" below).

QUARTERLY RESULTS

Many practitioners still show the required quarterly numbers in the footnotes, far removed from the discussion of the past two years. Logic and convenience require the data be located in the MD&A. The same considerations suggest that the data be keyed to that furnished in the variance table and to segment information, which also belongs in the MD&A not in a footnote, as shown in Exhibit 6.

EXHIBIT 6
Quarterly Results

Year One	1st Quarter $Amt	%Sales	2nd Quarter $Amt	%Sales	3rd Quarter $Amt	%Sales	4th Quarter $Amt	%Sales
			Net Sales					
Segment 1	3.3	50	3.4	49	4.4	50	5.4	50
Segment 2	2.2	33	2.3	33	3.3	37	4.3	39
Segment 3	1.1	27	1.2	18	1.2	13	1.2	11
	6.6	100	6.9	100	8.9	100	10.9	100
			Gross Income					
Segment 1	1.8	55	1.9	56	2.5	57	3.4	58
Segment 2	1.0	48	1.1	48	1.6	48	2.1	48
Segment 3	.6	52	.6	50	.6	48	.5	44
	3.4	51	3.6	52	4.7	53	6.0	55
			Operating Income					
Segment 1	.7	20	.7	21	1.0	22	1.2	23
Segment 2	.4	18	.4	18	.6	18	.8	18
Segment 3	.2	18	.2	17	.2	16	.2	15
	1.3	20	1.3	19	1.8	20	2.2	20
			Net Income					
	.5	8	.5	8	.8	9	1.1	10

CASH FLOW SUMMARY

The Financial Accounting Standards Board now requires companies to discard, as of 1988, the traditional sources and uses statement, which balances to change in working capital, in favor of a cash flow statement that shows the change in cash and equivalents as the sum of cash from operations, net financings, and net investments. The new presentation has long been sought by investment professionals. The required MD&A discussion of liquidity and capital resources should be accompanied by a summary table, as shown in Exhibit 7.

EXHIBIT 7
Cash Flow Summary ($ millions)

	5-Year Total	Year 5	Year 4	Year 3	Year 2	Year 1
From operations	15.0	5.0	4.0	3.0	2.0	1.0
Dividends	(1.5)	(.5)	(.4)	(.3)	(.2)	(.1)
Net investments	(8.8)	(1.0)	(5.0)	(4.0)	1.0	.2
Net financings	4.5	(1.0)	0.5	10.0	(3.0)	(2.0)
Change in cash & equivalent	9.2	2.5	(.9)	8.7	(.2)	(.9)

SHAREHOLDER INFORMATION

Assemble on one page all the information required related specifically to shares and shareholders. Add to that required minimum other information to help the owners of the business evaluate the past results of stock ownership, such as

- EPS, dividends, book value, price range, and volume for past eight quarters.
- EPS variance table for the past two years, as shown in Exhibit 5.
- Total return on investment, calculated for the past 5 and the past 10 years, compared with S&P, before and after inflation.
- A graphic illustration of business process, as shown in Exhibit 1.

- Annual meeting information and 10-K offering may be included, but should also be repeated on the inside front or rear.
- Dividend reinvestment and stock purchase programs detail.
- Nonobjecting beneficial holders direct mail instructions.
- Dividend policy discussion.

SEGMENT INFORMATION

Segment results for a company selling to a variety of markets or line-of-products information are vital to investors. The refusal by some companies to furnish them is both perplexing and frustrating to investors.

Segment, line-of-business, and class-of-product information reduces investors' risk and decision time. Expansion of the data and analysis is the most persistent and vociferous demand of investment professionals, who have now been heard by the SEC, which has new rules under consideration.

Tabular material of the type shown in Exhibit 8 has been

EXHIBIT 8
Segment Data

	Year 5	Year 4	Year 3	Year 2	Year 1
Sales ($ millions)					
1	23.3	22.1	21.2	20.9	19.2
2	27.2	22.5	17.6	14.1	12.4
3	25.0	25.0	24.0	23.8	24.0
Total	75.5	69.6	62.8	58.8	55.6
Pretax Income ($millions)					
1	3.0	2.9	2.8	3.0	2.7
2	4.1	3.3	2.3	1.7	1.3
3	2.6	2.6	2.5	2.5	2.5
Operating profit	9.7	8.9	7.6	7.2	6.5
Corporate & other expense	(2.7)	(2.9)	(2.5)	(2.4)	(2.2)

EXHIBIT 8 Segment Data *Continued*

	Year 5	Year 4	Year 3	Year 2	Year 1
Pretax income	7.0	6.0	5.1	4.8	4.3
Identifiable Assets ($ millions)					
1	11.1	12.0	8.1	7.7	6.8
2	9.4	9.0	8.0	7.4	7.3
3	11.4	11.9	10.9	11.3	10.9
Subtotal	31.9	30.1	27.0	26.4	25.0
Corporate & other	4.0	5.8	3.7	3.6	3.5
Total	35.9	35.9	30.7	30.0	28.5
Pretax Margin (% sales)					
1	12.8	12.9	13.2	14.1	14.2
2	15.2	14.6	13.1	12.0	10.6
3	10.5	10.6	10.4	10.5	10.6
Operating margin	12.8	12.7	12.1	12.2	11.7
Corporate overhead	(3.5)	(4.2)	(4.0)	(4.1)	(3.9)
Pretax margin	9.3	8.5	8.1	8.1	7.8
Asset Turnover (beginning)					
1	2.1x	2.4x	2.6x	2.7x	2.8x
2	2.9	2.5	2.2	1.9	1.7
3	2.2	2.1	2.2	2.1	2.2
Total asset turnover	2.1x	2.1x	2.0x	2.0x	1.9x

commended for its utility in understanding the parts of and developing growth prospects for the simplest or the most complex company.

CREDITORS' INFORMATION AND ANALYSIS

When a company goes bankrupt, it becomes clear there are more owners than just the stockholders. Creditors have special needs and interests which should be considered in developing MD&A text and tables. Such additional information could include:

- Times-interest-earned data.
- Fixed-charge coverage.

- Receivables turnover and/or aging.
- Inventory turnover.
- Goodwill amortization.

HISTORIC FINANCIAL DATA

It's axiomatic that investors require information for at least the past 6, preferably the past 11 years, for computing 5- and 10-year compound rates of change. The specific information should include more than "the numbers" — more than merely the dollar amounts from the financial statements. Exhibit 9 includes per-share data, cash flow information, and an ROE summary footing to a sustainable growth rate.

EXHIBIT 9 Financial Summary

	Year 6	Year 5	Year 4	Year 3	Year 2	Year 1
Per-Share Data ($)						
Sales	15.69	12.85	10.98	8.53	7.89	7.05
Assets	8.45	6.47	5.33	3.96	2.85	2.12
Equity	5.69	4.01	2.95	2.28	1.53	.73
Earnings	1.11	.90	.67	.69	.54	.49
Dividends	.10	.05	—	—	—	—
Price: high	21.88	12.75	11.88	17.12	11.06	10.0
Price: low	11.88	7.88	7.06	10.50	3.38	6.0
PE range: high	21.2	17.2	17.7	24.8	20.5	20.1
PE range: low	11.5	10.6	10.5	15.2	6.2	10.2
Income Data ($ millions)						
Net sales	257.5	198.3	168.9	131.2	112.6	92.3
Operating income	35.9	26.7	19.1	18.4	13.7	8.8
Net other income & expenses	1.0	.2	(.7)	.8	.6	.2
Pretax income	36.9	26.9	18.4	19.2	14.3	9.0
Income taxes	18.7	13.0	8.1	8.6	6.6	4.1
Net income	18.2	13.9	10.3	10.6	7.7	4.9
Shares outstanding	16.4	15.4	15.4	15.4	14.3	13.1

EXHIBIT 9 **Financial Summary** *Continued*

	Year 6	Year 5	Year 4	Year 3	Year 2	Year 1
Balance Sheet Data ($ millions)						
Current assets	59.9	36.3	21.5	29.7	26.7	16.2
Net fixed assets	68.0	55.6	51.9	28.2	15.4	10.7
Total assets	139.3	98.7	80.5	59.4	42.5	25.6
Current liabilities	36.1	30.5	31.1	22.5	17.7	16.6
Long-term debt	.4	.4	.7	.1	.7	.8
Stockholders' equity	93.8	61.2	44.6	34.3	22.8	9.5
Funds Flow Data ($ millions)						
From operations	36.3	36.5	20.8	17.7	11.5	7.6
Dividends	1.5	0.7	—	—	—	—
Used for investment	(33.8)	(16.4)	(40.0)	(18.4)	(6.8)	(3.7)
From financing	13.9	(6.7)	7.9	.4	3.8	(2.4)
Change cash & equivalents	14.9	12.7	(11.3)	(.3)	8.5	1.5
Ratio Analysis						
Operating margin	13.9%	13.5%	11.3%	14.0%	12.1%	9.5%
Pretax margin	14.3	13.6	10.9	14.6	12.7	9.8
Effective tax rate	50.7	48.4	44.1	44.8	46.0	45.2
Net margin	7.1	7.0	6.1	8.1	6.9	5.4
Asset turnover*	2.61x	2.46x	2.84x	3.09x	4.07x	4.12x
Return on assets*	18.53%	17.22%	17.32%	25.03x	28.08x	22.25
Financial leverage*	1.61x	1.81x	1.73x	1.86x	2.91x	5.40x
Return on equity*	29.83%	31.17%	29.96%	46.56%	81.71%	120.15%
Retention rate	92%	95%	100%	100%	100%	100%
Implied growth rate	27%	29%	30%	47%	82%	120%

*Beginning.

HISTORIC INDUSTRY DATA

Some analysts begin the investment decision process at the industry level and work down to the company. Others begin with the company and work up to the industry. Such information is not often widely available. Providing industry data may not only compress the decision timespan, but foster management credibility as well.

GRAPHIC PRINCIPLES

Almost any attention to the graphic appearance of the MD&A, including the statements and notes, can greatly improve the visual appeal of these, the most daunting sections of the annual report. In choosing the graphic treatment and selecting from the myriad graphic elements, bear in mind that the intention is to inform, not to dazzle or amuse. Four-color, captionless product pictures in the empty space under the income statement do carry a message and lend a dash of color. So does a five-year sales chart in the margin near the discussion of last year's results. But without complete captions, the message delivered may not be the one intended. Light gray pebble-grain paper may separate the front from the back, but it may be harder to read and be taken as a warning that "the financials" are boring and unimportant.

The second principle is that a well-executed MD&A requires a close working relationship between the several interests involved: investor relations, accounting, legal, and design/printing. No one is skilled or informed enough to develop and execute a coherent financial discussion, illustrated by charts, photos, captions, headings, etc., which all combine to deliver the desired result — an informed and interested reader.

Third, reinforcement is the key to memory. The various aspects of a message must be delivered several times, in several ways. *Topical subheadings* can be used to present an outline of the main points that comprise the overall message. That outline reinforces some or all of the message every time the reader turns a page, or moves forward or backward through the book. *Charts and pictures with captions* should comprise an information packet independent of the copy on the page, which may mention or elaborate on the subject of the information packet.

Finally, the audience is smarter and more demanding than conventional wisdom admits. Do not be misled by one perennial finding of the many annual report surveys — the letter to shareholders is the "most read" part of the book. There are two large and influential audiences who use the entire book in making their decisions: the swelling ranks of portfolio managers and the growing army of individual investors who are serious about their money.

* * * * *

LeRoy A. Glasner, Jr., is senior partner of The Financial Relations Board, Inc. He is considered the investor relations industry's leading advocate of advancing the informational content of corporate disclosure statements.